Gary Goodman's
60-Second Salesperson

Dr. Gary S. Goodman, an internationally recognized consultant, seminar leader, and media personality, is the president of Goodman Communications Corporation, whose clients include Xerox Corporation, Polaroid, Flying Tigers, General Foods, Abbott Laboratories, and many of the Fortune 500 companies as well as nonprofit organizations. He is also the author of four Prentice-Hall bestsellers, *You Can Sell Anything by Telephone!, Selling Skills for the Nonsalesperson, Reach Out and Sell Someone,* and *Winning by Telephone.*

Gary Goodman's 60-Second Salesperson

Dr. Gary S. Goodman

A SPECTRUM BOOK

Prentice-Hall, Inc.,
Englewood Cliffs, New Jersey 07632

Library of Congress Cataloging in Publication Data

Goodman, Gary S.
    Gary Goodman's 60-second salesperson.

    "A Spectrum Book."
    Includes index.
    1. Telephone selling.   I. Goodman, Gary S. 60-second
salespersoon.   II. Title.
HF5438.3.G65   1985   658.8'5   84-26447
ISBN 0-13-346883-6
ISBN 0-13-346875-5 (pbk.)

1 2 3 4 5 6 7 8 9 10

ISBN 0-13-346883-6

ISBN 0-13-346875-5 {PBK.}

Editorial/production supervision by Rhonda K. Mirabella
Cover design ©1985 by Jeannette Jacobs
Manufacturing buyer: Carol Bystrom

This book is available at a special discount when ordered in
bulk quantities. Contact Prentice-Hall, Inc., General
Publishing Division, Special Sales, Englewood Cliffs, N.J. 07632.

Prentice-Hall International, Inc., *London*
Prentice-Hall of Australia Pty. Limited, *Sydney*
Prentice-Hall Canada Inc., *Toronto*
Prentice-Hall Hispanoamericana, S.A., *Mexico*
Prentice-Hall of India Private Limited, *New Delhi*
Prentice-Hall of Japan, Inc., *Tokyo*
Prentice-Hall of Southeast Asia Pte. Ltd., *Singapore*
Whitehall Books Limited, *Wellington, New Zealand*
Editora Prentice-Hall do Brasil Ltda., *Rio de Janeiro*

This book is dedicated to my wife, best friend, and colleague, Dr. Deanne Honeyman-Goodman, to the warm memories of my father, Bernard Goodman, and to Roy Honeyman.

Contents

Preface

If you were given only sixty seconds to open and close an important sale, could you do it?

This is the challenge of *Gary Goodman's 60-Second Salesperson*. Through this book you'll see how to make every second count as you learn how to master the telemarketing process that is revolutionizing the way modern firms are doing business.

Specifically, you'll learn to:

- Psych yourself up before you get on the phone.
- Build rapport with strangers within the first ten seconds of the sales talk.
- Establish your credibility in the next ten seconds.
- Create desire for your products and services.
- Construct appealing offers.
- Engineer commitment.
- Seal the deal.

All within 60 seconds.

I know you're going to like this book, and I hope you'll find that it becomes one of your most practical tools for increasing your sales performance.

Gary Goodman's
60-Second Salesperson

1

Your 60-Second Psych-up

Do you like self-help books? I'm really hooked on them because they not only give me a boost when I need it most; they also turn me on to my own potential.

Before we can become 60-second salespeople, we need to explore the psychodynamics of success and failure in selling. Perhaps the best way to begin is to look into the reasons why so many of us are assured to fail instead of succeed.

Several years ago, I ran across a psychology book that had a captivating title that has haunted me ever since I first laid eyes on it. The title? *Man Against Himself* (Karl Menninger. N.Y.: Harcourt Brace Jovanovich, 1938, revised ed., N.Y.: Harcourt Brace, 1966). Wow! There is great wisdom in those three words. If I were to write that book today, I might call it *Salesman Against Himself*, because I firmly believe that we place more obstacles in our own paths than do all the forces of other people and of nature.

This chapter is devoted to identifying and overcoming those occupational maladies that afflict salespeople. Once we have cured these, we'll examine the telemarketing process 10 seconds at a time, learning along the way how you can create rapport, project your credibility, describe products and services attractively, fashion an irresistible offer, create commitment, and seal the deal—all within 60 seconds.

Many of us defeat ourselves by postponing actions that would make us successful if we simply completed them. In short, we *procrastinate.* Instead of exploiting every moment as a precious resource, we squander our time worrying about failure, rationalizing, or daydreaming about success instead of providing for it.

Why do we procrastinate to begin with? Some of the basic causes of putting off important things are discussed in the following several pages.

1. *Low frustration tolerance.* When projects seem as though they are going to take a long time to complete, many of us find it very uncomfortable to wait to see them through. One cause of our impatience is usually some kind of belief that we foster about how "awful" it is to deal with prospects who beat around the bush and take a long time in their decision-making process.

2. *Fear of failure.* Failure tends to be painful for most of us who have been raised by parents and teachers to be winners in everything we do. Instead of seeing failure as a temporary setback on the road to ultimate success, people can see it as devastating feedback that says, "Look, you're really not cut out for this type of thing, so just pack it up right here." AMOCO, the oil giant, discovers more new oil wells than any other company. How come? *They drill more wells!* It's that simple. Another way of looking at AMOCO's success is to infer that the company is more tolerant of failure than its competitors. It would have to be to put up with the number of dry wells that it inevitably discovers in addition to the profitable ones. If our fear of failure is stronger than our drive to succeed, we'll sit on our hands and wait for a better opportunity to fall from the sky.

3. *Perfectionism.* This is a sneaky little gremlin. How many of us have known someone who puts off doing something until "everything is just right"? People who delay doing things because they insist that circumstances be ideal for performing the task are really not so quality-conscious as they may appear. They are probably afraid of a poor showing, and if they can delay having to perform they may never have to run the risk of losing face.

4. *Fear of rejection.* Being liked by others is an important motive for many salespeople. In fact, "liking people" is one of the main reasons people decide to enter the sales profession. It is a "people business." This motivation can boomerang on you if you come to regard being liked as more important than being successful.

Let's say that you have known a client for some time and you have come to feel pretty close to the person. If you are like many sellers, you may come to feel "a little guilty" about putting the proposal to the client and asking for the business directly. If you were dealing with a total stranger, you would feel no hesitation whatsoever. But in working with someone who knows you on a personal basis you may feel that you would rather withstand the pain of having one less sale than have to confront the withdrawal of your client's esteem or affection. If this is happening to you, you are probably telling yourself that "friendship is more important than sales," or something of the sort. What you really feel is the fear of being rejected by someone significant, and we often take great measures to avoid this outcome.

5. *Complacency.* If you aren't careful, you can lull yourself into a veritable stupor by accepting a certain level of success as being normal and comfortable.

Yesterday I was speaking to a very successful salesperson who is way ahead of his peers in selling computer equipment. He has set a goal of earning $250,000 per year, which is a rather ambitious target for him. Right now, he is really hungering for that juicy reward because he can visualize all of the tasty treats that will be in store: a nicer home at the beach, a racier car to have fun in and with which to impress prospects, and enough pocket money to satisfy every whim. He is in good shape right now, from a psychological standpoint. His real problems will begin when his financial target starts getting closer to his grasp. This is the point at which many salespeople start their long and steady decline into mediocrity.

As you get closer to your goals you can lose that sharpness of attitude and outlook that motivates you to keep trying. It becomes easier and easier to allow yourself to look backward at how far you've come, and to be satisfied with what you see behind you, instead of revising your goals to make your future look challenging, compelling, and inviting.

6. *Fear of experimenting.* I think scientists are potentially great salespeople in at least a few respects. They tend to look at what they are learning less emotionally than the rest of us, and this helps them to learn very efficiently. For instance, let's say a scientist wants to learn about the temperature at which water boils. (Assume, of course, that this wasn't already known.)

How would the person proceed? He or she would start with a pot of water, a continuously burning flame, and a thermometer. Through observation and meticulous measurement, he or she would then determine when the water began to vaporize.

If she spilled some water on the way to the stove, she probably wouldn't chastise herself and refuse to carry on the experiment; she'd probably refill the pot and begin again. If she had guessed or hypothesized that the water would boil at 200 degrees, but found that this temperature failed to cause the desired effect, she wouldn't moan and groan but would instead allow the data to cause a revision of her initial guess. She'd keep trying until she found what she was looking for, altering her strategy as required by changing circumstances.

The typical salesperson would not have the patience to methodically explore the process that would yield the most favorable results. Instead, he or she would probably be satisfied to know what didn't work, while giving up in the pursuit of what did.

A scientist attempts to avoid becoming ego-involved with what is being studied. This is very helpful because he will not favor one sort of explanation over another simply because he "likes it" or "is comfortable with it."

I have encountered numerous sellers who insist upon doing things in certain ways for these very reasons, and they contend that their rationale is completely justified.

When you adopt an experimental frame of mind, you set into motion the kinds of forces that smash through your habits of procrastination. By "trying anything," you undertake the most difficult part of any enterprise: the *beginning*.

This is in keeping with the statement that some successful sales managers make: "I don't care what you do; just do something!" As these leaders know, some activity, no matter how apparently random, invariably leads to more concerted efforts.

7. *The need to be right all the time.* Imagine never being able to make a mistake. What a terrible way to live!

I fall into this trap as a consultant. As an advisor to thousands of people, and perhaps millions if I add my media audiences, I can easily come to feel "that I should do no wrong," and I can start viewing my career this way, at least when it comes to the sales process. What does this do to my abilities? I become less likely to get back to the selling process because I am afraid of making a mistake as this would show me to be "wrong," at least on occasion, which might threaten my self-image as a knowledgeable consultant.

Because I am aware of this tendency I can arrest it in its early stages and avoid falling victim to it. As a result, I am less likely to procrastinate.

I often tell sales trainees to "make a lot of mistakes" as I recognize their defensiveness about being newly trained, and their associated feelings of wanting to be right all the time. Sometimes I'll even hang a poster in a sales meeting room that reads: "It is better to be rich than to be right."

8. *Unrealistic expectations.* What happens when you have inflated expectations that don't work out? If you are like most, you become disenchanted very quickly and promise yourself that you won't make the mistake of setting your hopes as high as you did the first time.

Unrealistic expectations lead to impulsiveness and impulsive actions lead to failure. When you fail you become "gun-shy," which prevents you from trying again when you need to.

What you tend to do is wait until you can have unrealistically high expectations for succeeding, jump in on impulse, and jump out as quickly as you ventured in.

If you look at circumstances realistically, and carefully assess the requirements for succeeding, you become less dazzled by your hopes for instant gains and sobered by the work challenge before you. Then, if you undertake the task, you are prepared to weather the psychological storms that inevitably come from an involved project.

9. *Fear of success.* Some of us are actually afraid of succeeding because positive results cause others to expect us to succeed in the future. In fact, it is likely that other folks would expect even more dramatic results from our future efforts.

Instead of risking the pressure that could come with success, a number of us retreat into procrastination, which provides a temporary respite from the expectations of others.

10. *Habits.* Do you always wait until the very last minute to undertake a project because you tell yourself "I work best under pressure"?

If you do, you are kidding yourself. You are also trying to insulate yourself from the shock of failing because you can always tell yourself that you did a rush job, and how could anyone expect better results under such circumstances?

When you postpone important things habitually, you create a stress cycle that can add a tremendous burden to your already challenging responsibilities. Sooner or later, something will break down, and it can be your track record or even your health.

Reward Yourself
When You Deserve It

A great way to overcome procrastination is to set up a reward structure for yourself that reinforces the right kinds of take-charge behaviors.

For instance, let's say that you need to do some telephone prospecting because you realize that the cultivation of a number of contacts will ultimately lead to closing new business. Make a scorecard for yourself, and on it place your target number of contacts. Let's say that you have a goal to reach fifty new prospects today. To do so, you will need to make 130 calls, allowing for screening, people at lunch, and people who are otherwise unavailable.

Assume that you can make 19 calls per hour, yielding approximately 6.25 contacts with decision makers per hour, or 50 for your eight-hour day.

After each hour that you are on target in terms of results, give yourself a reward such as a coffee break. When you have reached your magic number of fifty contacts, pat yourself on the back and treat yourself to something nice, like a special dinner or an evening out.

You'll find that you become eager to continue your work under these circumstances because you have created a reward system that keeps you at the grindstone but mercifully rewards you for shouldering your responsibilities.

Punishments Work, Too ...

What happens if you chronically miss your targets? Most of us just shrug off this kind of dissappointment and hope that tomorrow will be a better day. However, hoping isn't always enough to create and sustain behavioral change.

Gruesome as it may sound, we need to discourage our negative behavior through some sort of punishment. We need to make doing the right thing comfortable and doing the wrong thing very uncomfortable.

What do I have in mind? For starters, you might consider making a little deal with yourself. For each day that you fail to make your targets, you might force yourself to do something that would enhance the position of your competitors. If they sell modestly priced products, buy some. Or make a charitable donation in their name.

Whatever you decide to do, it should be somewhat painful, from a psychological standpoint. You may even consider giving money to a despised political cause.

Once you have decided on your punishments, by all means follow through with them. You'll find that your behavior will come into line very quickly if you follow these guidelines.

Make Selling a Game—
and Prepare to Win

Selling is a fun game when you think about it. Through the selling process, we're able to match wits with the powerful and the foolish, depending on who we're speaking to at the given time.

Truly great salespeople look at the sales process as a fun-filled contest where they are constantly strategizing and making calculated moves. Some work, and others, well ...

And that's a part of the fun. We never know with 100 percent certainty what techniques or appeals will turn a customer on or miss the mark altogether.

One of the best parts of the selling situation is that you get a chance to measure your effectiveness. Think of how few occupations offer this kind of reward. Can dental hygienists, important as their work is, feel comfortable that they have vastly surpassed their previous day's efforts? What about comparing today's achievement with the level you reached one year ago? Is there any objective standard of measurement that lends itself to capturing and comparing such performances over time? Not really. But there are in selling, because in this game you can measure results in "yesses" and in dollars. If you want to see how you're doing from month to month, all you have to do is scrutinize your paycheck stubs. They'll tell you the whole story.

This is very exciting, because you can see yourself growing and moving forward. If you wish to really take off, there is nothing standing in your way, either.

The Art of Goal Setting

Every course on time management seems to contain a very important unit on goal setting, and for a good reason. If you fail to make your goals known to yourself and explicit, you won't reach them.

Even if we are used to setting goals, most of us do so all too shortsightedly. Panasonic is one company that is anything but shortsighted, though. The folks in their office-systems division have put together a *250-year research and development plan* because they don't believe in jumping into things without exploring all the implications!

While this may be a little far out for most of us, who don't have enough patience to span a couple of centuries, there is a lesson to be learned in the Panasonic example. Simply speaking, six-month, one-year, and five-year plans may not be long enough to really be motivational. Sometimes we need to see things in a larger perspective in order to fully realize our potential.

Dare to Dream Big!

Before you go about the business of selling, pause to visualize what you are striving for. Is it a better car, or a more beautiful place in which to live? Or a tennis court with a swimming pool to keep it company? Or a 'round-the-world cruise replete with full-time entertainment and interesting cruisemates?

Whatever it is that you are striving for, do yourself a mighty favor and make sure that it justifies your effort. I say this because only highly motivational dreams will catalyze the resources inside of you that are needed for encouraging fulfillment.

Robert Schuller, the charismatic minister and founder of the Crystal Cathedral in California, observes that people love to be a part of big projects. Big undertakings are motivating because they inspire us to greater heights, while less ambitious projects are often consigned to obscurity, because few people wish to be bothered with the trivial.

See Your Dream
in "Living Color"

Visualizing what you want is quite important, as well. I remember growing up with a very good friend named Bobby who was a good athlete. We used to pal around together, so it wasn't surprising that we tried out for Little League at the same time.

I remember Bobby telling me that he hoped we'd make the same team because he was a pitcher and I was a catcher, and we could simply keep practicing together as we had in the past.

As things turned out, he made the Cardinals and I made the Dodgers. I remember saying to him when we got the results that I promised to hit a home run off of him the first time I came to bat against him, and I made a point of insisting that the "shot" would be placed directly over the center-field wall.

"Sure, Goodman; no way," he said. Well, it wasn't until two years later that I had my chance to "put up or shut up." The situation was tense, as it was a close game and I was about to come to bat. All of a sudden, Bobby was brought in as a relief pitcher, and I remember watching him take his warm-up throws.

In my mind I repeated the scene I had mentally rehearsed hundreds of times: The pitch coming in on the outside corner of the plate, tailing off away from me as a fastball does when thrown by a left-hander like Bobby.

As I was being announced I stepped next to the batter's box and slyly pointed to center field, as the great Babe Ruth had reportedly done in his day. I recall my friend barely cracked a smile and shook his head as if to say, "There's no way I'm going to go along with *that*!"

I stepped up and the first pitch was a Ball. The next was a Ball. The third pitch was just as I had dreamed: a fastball tailing away quickly at the outside corner.

Time seemed to freeze as my mind computed the trajectory of the pitch. I knew this was the one. Suddenly I let go and leaned into the ball; the next thing I sensed was the crack of the bat.

It didn't have that "I-know-this-one's-gone" sound, but the ball was hit in the right place, center field, and it was sky-high. It seemed like hours waiting for it to start its descent. I slowly navigated my way around first base waiting for the thing to dive downward.

It started sloping, sloping—it looked long enough—it was *gone!* A home run, and exactly as I had dreamed it. Well, not exactly. My dreams hadn't kept me in this kind of suspense! Nevertheless, it was beautiful. Bobby just watched and shook his head in disbelief.

The curious thing about this experience and others like it is the fact that in my heart of hearts I didn't think events could have been otherwise. It just had to turn out this way.

This is the way to dream. *See all of the details.* If you are setting your sights on a beautiful home, imagine what the yard will look like. Take yourself on a tour of the grounds. Smell the flowers. Where will the doghouse be?

It may sound silly, but only when you become detailed in your dreams do you make them come true. Only then do they stop being mere wishes.

I went to graduate school with a fellow who has created a fascinating business: he teaches businesspeople to laugh while helping them to develop their sense of humor.

Sound foolish? According to numbers of sources, laughter is just the right tonic for many ills, including sluggish sales. When people are laughing, their sales resistance diminishes and they tend to see the world more optimistically.

I remember sitting next to comedian Marty Allen on a flight from San Francisco to Los Angeles a few years back, and we had a very interesting conversation. I wanted to know something about his philosphy of humor and discover what he thought was really funny.

He talked about the characters he creates and how slapstick tends to be his staple. When I asked him how I might heighten the humor I use in seminars, he recommended the public library as a source of expert advice on the subject.

"The library?" I asked.

"Sure. There are some great books on humor there."

"And you mean to tell me you've used them?"

"Of course. Everyone does."

Good advice. There's one other thing we should remember when it comes to humor. *Tell yourself some jokes!* That's right, have a good time with yourself.

Do you remember times when you were a schoolkid and suddenly something struck you as so funny you could hardly keep from splitting your sides? I'll bet you can't recall too many of the stimuli that struck you this way, but they were funny enough at the time to make you wonder if you were ever going to catch your breath.

Everything around us is funny. I remember going into the Department of Motor Vehicles to get a replacement license because mine had become so battered it was unrecognizable. I don't know what it was about the place, but *everything* was outrageously funny.

People working there seemed to take themselves *so seriously.* The fellow who was obviously the big cheese would strut in and out of his office for no apparent reason but to flirt with a buxom clerk who looked as if she had emerged from a Fifties skit.

The woman who took the mug shots was a real sweetheart: She'd nicely encourage each applicant to "smile" before she took the picture; to make things easier, she would make a big grin herself for people to imitate.

Something came over me as I watched this ritual of person after person being verbally and nonverbally encouraged. Instead of smiling, what if she suddenly made monster faces at the people who were lined up so politely? Would they imitate her and get stuck with a grotesque grin on their licenses?

I don't know, but this sort of mindless speculation had me cracking up, and it sure took the dullness out of the process of getting my i.d.

Develop Confidence in Yourself

One of the greatest obstacles to success is an inadequate self-image. Deep down, or maybe not so deep down, we don't feel very good about our abilities. And this negativity can be painful and very inhibiting unless we learn to hold it at bay and supply ourselves with positive feelings about ourselves.

A number of people claim that our feelings of inadequacy are implanted by parents and teachers who encourage us to feel weak and stupid, and who reward us for being dependent, while chastising us when we show signs of independence.

No matter what their source, by the time we mature we tend to "own" these feelings, and we see them as being completely natural and accurate reflections of our true essence. Worse still, we reinforce the negatives by repeating them and by allowing others to broadcast them to us.

I'll give you a recent example of what I'm talking about. Yesterday a person called me from a remote area of the country and purchased one of my other books, *Reach Out & Sell Someone*. She had read *Selling Skills for the Nonsalesperson* and wanted more information on what I had labeled as "phone fear." She said, "You see, I suffer from phone fear."

I'm confident that this was an accurate description of her past experience: She *had* suffered from phone fear.

If she were truly a friend to herself she would have phrased her problem in a slightly different fashion. She would have said, "I *have suffered* from phone fear." This would have made her feel that she was about to put that behind her and change her life, but by placing the problem in the present she may have inadvertently given it a future life.

We do this kind of subtle sabotage to ourselves all the time, and we allow others to do it to us. Spouses can put each other in conceptual cages after a while by insisting that the other person is *always* doing such and such, or *never* doing something else, or is *totally incapable* of being different in one way or other.

After hearing these claims from the lips of other people we are inclined not only to believe these assertions, but to repeat them to ourselves at critical times, thus de-skilling ourselves.

Let's say that I have an inadequate self-image when it comes to repairing items around the house. All of a sudden calamity strikes, and a pipe breaks in the basement and water starts gushing forth. If I am insecure I'll probably panic and not be able to take stock of the situation and dispassionately do what needs to be done. I may even mentally thrash myself for "never knowing anything about these kinds of things," which can lead to further self-recrimination and an impulse to avoid learning about fix-it subjects in the future, which will create more self-denigration, and so on.

To arrest and reverse this negative cycle, we need to unlearn the habit of *putting ourselves down*. The first step is to alter the language we use with ourselves to describe our experience.

Frankly, many of us are too punitive with ourselves when we should be critical of the behavior patterns that aren't getting us what we want. I am not an *awful person* because I have not been effective in home repairs in the past. I have simply not been effective in forming appropriate home-repair behavior patterns. Clearly, if I want to change the results I get around the house, I should change my non-behavior or ineffective behavior into effective behavior.

However, I don't have to radically change myself!

If I perceived the ineffectiveness in the arena of home repair as being a problem with *me*, I would be very reluctant to change anything in my behavior because this would be dramatic evidence of my past ineptitude, or so it would appear to me from a psychological viewpoint. Therefore, in doing nothing, I am not admitting the guilt I feel for being incompetent in home improvement. This is one of the only means I have for retaining a sense of positive self-regard in this circumstance.

Remember, the behavior may be "bad," but we aren't. Our selling strategies may be ineffective in certain settings, but this doesn't make us ineffective as *people*.

Think of your behavior as a set of tools. Some tools fit some tasks and don't fit others. This doesn't make them "good" or "bad" tools but simply useful or less useful.

When the Going Gets Tough, Remember Your Successes

I am going to ask you to spend sixty seconds and make a list of the ten things that you have accomplished in your life of which you are most proud.

These may not be the things that your spouse or parents or business associates would list as being meaningful to them. They don't count here; only you do.

After you make your list, we'll discuss the importance of this exercise. By the way, you don't have to rank the items. Simply write them down as they pop into your mind.

You probably have a lot more to be proud of then you thought. What is it about all of the things you listed that seems to be a common thread?

I'll bet that most of your successes came after you experienced

1. A challenge or problem.
2. Self-doubt.
3. A commitment to do your best.

Which of the three items listed here do you think we most often forget when we recall our past glories? That's right, step number 2, or self-doubt.

When we are about to take on a truly challenging task we

always experience at least a little anxiety and worry about the outcome. This is the time when we need to be most aware of our feelings so we can summon the gumption to move forward with great energy, even though we have no assurance of ultimate success.

The next time you get that empty feeling in your stomach and you feel almost woozy under the burden of the task you have set before you, whether it is to go after a bigger client than you ever have before or to take a risk in some aspect of your sales presentation, pull out your list of successes and remind yourself of this very important idea:

> "Look at what I've accomplished! I did it then, and I'm even more capable now. In fact, compared to the magnitude of challenges that I used to face, this one is a piker!"

> "Someday, I'll look upon this experience as having been very instructive and helpful to me."

> "I'm really going to enjoy this venture!"

And a Certain Amount of Humility Helps, Too

We're all learning all the time, if we are open to our experiences. This is really important to remember, because we may suffer through seemingly disastrous setbacks and emerge from them with renewed vitality and insight and become literally "unstoppable" in our quest for success when we get started again. We may do so only if we learn to punctuate our experience properly, and give it the right interpretation.

What's so bad about failing? Nothing, if you see it simply as a learning experience that is designed to show you a better path. Learn to shake off your setbacks, as ballplayers and other athletes learn to shake off minor injuries, and jump right back into the contest.

On the other hand, if you tell yourself that you "should know it all by now," you'll tend to make your shortcomings major ego-blows that will soon have you reeling on the ropes, if not down for the count. Be humble, and remind yourself, "I'm learning new things every day, and I'm going to enjoy the feeling of freedom that comes from not having to know it all."

Your 60-Second Psych-up

Repeat these statements to yourself before you start your selling day, and you'll find you give your mind a quick and effective tune-up:

1. I am going to overcome procrastination and do what needs to be done right away.
2. I will increase my frustration tolerance so that I may persevere in the face of minor irritations. I will not sacrifice long-term goals for short-term diversions and satisfactions.
3. I will accept failure merely as corrective feedback that is designed to help me improve. Failing is, simply, learning.
4. I will not be a perfectionist. I will learn to move forward without total confidence and assurance.
5. I will stay motivated and avoid complacency.
6. I will become much more experimental and have fun while trying new strategies.
7. I will not try to be "right" all the time.
8. I will set forth realistic but challenging expectations for my own performance.
9. I will not fear success, but feel confident that my continuing success will teach me ways of becoming increasingly successful in the future. I have yet to realize my greatest successes.
10. I will change my work habits to conform to what proves to be maximally rewarding. I will set up a system of rewards and punishments that will shape my behavior constructively.
11. I will dream bigger, visualizing the details of a better life for myself and those I love.
12. I'll develop my sense of humor, and strive to see the lighter side of even the darkest situations.
13. I'll develop self-confidence and avoid putting myself down. I'll appreciate that my behavior may be inefficient, and that it can be changed. I will always be a good person, no matter how efficiently I am acting at a given time.
14. When the going gets tough, I'll remind myself of my ten greatest successes, and I'll know that I'll be successful again and again. If I did it then, under even more trying circumstances, I can certainly do it now!

15. I will always remain humble to a certain extent, while acknowledging that I am continually learning; as long as I am, I am truly alive.

When you have mastered your outlook you will have stopped being against yourself and started the important process of poising yourself for sustained success. In the chapters to follow we'll discuss how you can build a winning telemarketing call, ten seconds at a time.

2

The First 10 Seconds
Building Rapport

All of us are sensitive to the fact that first impressions count quite a bit in determining how we are judged by other people. Some people take more care in composing themselves before a social or business transaction than others, though, and these people find that their efforts are nicely rewarded.

There is no question that we can and do make first impressions by telephone, and I can tell you with certainty that most of us come across very poorly through this medium.

In the first place, we have no idea of how we sound when we speak on the phone. How often have you had your voice tape-recorded as it sounds through a phone? Frequently? Seldom? Probably never, right? Right. And why not? Either you never gave it much serious thought, or you were afraid that you would be embarrassed by what you heard. Well, this concern isn't unusual, but if you expect to get the most out of your telephone calls you need to have an accurate reading of where you are starting from.

And there is nothing quite as revealing and honest as a cassette recording of your golden tones. When you begin to seriously study your telephone voice you'll be opening a new aspect of your sales consciousness that will reward you handsomely.

This chapter is dedicated to showing you how to achieve rapport within the first ten seconds of your telemarketing call. With rapport, you'll be on your way to numerous sales, but without it you'll be climbing uphill all the way.

What Prospects Like and Don't Like to Hear

Many salespeople have the wrong idea of what makes prospects comfortable. Ask some typical sellers what they do at the beginning of a call and they'll volunteer that they try to be very, very polite and unassuming. In this way, they'll be absolutely agreeable and the prospect won't feel that they are being overly aggressive or "pushy."

In other words, numbers of salespeople will tell you what they *don't* do at the beginning of a call and what they *avoid* sounding like. This seems fine and good until you scrutinize it with greater care.

It's very hard to not communicate. Have you ever tried it? I recall as a child promising my parents that I would "disappear" and "make myself invisible" when I felt besieged by some request to perform a chore when I wanted to run off and play ball, or something. (Little did I realize that they probably wished I could vaporize from time to time!)

Though I tried to pull off the Claude Rains/Invisible Man routine, nature conspired to keep me in my typical corporeal state. I simply couldn't disappear.

Similarly, it is extremely difficult for a salesperson to attempt to build an architecture of selling based upon the phantom foundation of what he or she is *not* going to seem like to another person. It's like "not communicating": Even if you think you're being coy and not making any statements, your silence is often interpreted as constituting a message, if only the fact that you don't care to speak at that particular moment.

Prospects don't respond well to overly polite people anyway, although many believe that "you can't be too polite."

Not true. In fact, excessive politeness really comes across as weakness on the part of the seller at the beginning of a call.

Prospects want to listen to people who can make them lis-

ten. They like people who have a sense of command in their voices and who are able to succinctly introduce themselves, their company, and their product or service.

For some people, a sense of command seems almost a part of them. For example, take my insurance man, Jim. He has been endowed with a voice that is deep, booming, resonant, and extremely attention-getting. If he would invest more time in telemarketing than he does at present, he'd find his business growing at an even faster clip than it is now.

In Jim's case, a golden voice and robust delivery seem to be innately endowed. The rest of us need to work at cultivating what seems to come naturally to him.

This isn't to say that there is only one particular type of voice that will produce rapport. Various sorts of voices will, as long as their "owners" do certain things with them.

Sound Like a Winner

I can label people as "winners" or "losers" simply by listening to the way they introduce themselves over the phone. I recognize this may not seem humanistic or charitable on my part, but the great majority of people I speak to simply don't "have it" when it comes to vocal style and dynamism.

What do I mean? I'll give you an example. I recently assisted a client in screening telemarketing applicants by phone. We wanted to invite only the most promising candidates to interviews for the purpose of time management.

I found that one in fifteen had the sort of delivery that was acceptable. That's right, one in fifteen! That's less than seven percent.

I knew beforehand that the odds weren't going to be that great at finding truly effective telecommunicators, but this was way beyond my expectations. How were these people deficient? Let me count the ways ...

1. *They sounded negative.* This is very common. People can inadvertently come across to others as if they were *blaming them* for what third parties had done to them in the past. Salespeople are famous for taking out their frustrations with past prospects when they are trying to sell present ones.

What is a negative voice? It's one that sounds downcast, where the ends of sentences trail off. Negative voices will sound unconvinced of the benefits they are presumably touting to the listener.

2. *They failed to articulate properly.* Clear and understandable speech is crucial to succeeding in telemarketing. Losers sound garbled. They employ what has been termed "sloppy speech." As I have maintained elsewhere, people judge others to be intelligent or otherwise mainly upon the quality of their diction. Sound slurred or sloppy and you'll come across like a dummy.

At the same time, I can't say enough for developing more effective speaking habits. When you are selling you are taking on a leadership role and you are trying to enlist the allegiance of the prospect. As with most people, prospects place more confidence in the person who seems crisp and verbally adept than in the everyday "street-talker" that many of us can sound like if we aren't careful.

3. *They expected me to carry the conversation for them.* There is a basic principle of effective communication that should be noted: *If you wish to get information from someone over the phone, you should first volunteer some information yourself.* In this manner you create a sense of trust which is a prerequisite for a productive conversation. In another section we'll discuss how you can "pass the ball" to someone else, but this must be done very smoothly, and only after you have announced your purpose and identification to the listener.

4. *They sounded immature.* I'd like to point out that "immature" is not a code word for "too young." I don't think you can be too young for a telemarketing job, as long as you sound businesslike and "solid."

I was discussing how some of the callers sounded with a telemarketing supervisor I had trained and she came up with a good description: "beachy." There seems to be a certain sound in the voices of teenagers and their immediate elders that is *chic* among that group. It's akin to the "Valley Girl" (and Boy) talk:

> "Ya know; I mean, like I'd really like you to, ya know, think hard about buying this thing, ya know?"

In addition to using this sort of language, with its start-again-stop-again quality, immature-sounding callers struggle to come across as being a little too "cool." Their tone suggests:

> "Buy or don't buy, I couldn't care less; I mean, ya know?"

5. *They used substandard English.* This is an increasing problem among young people, many of whom have been schooled in overly permissive or negligent situations.

There is no question that you need to sound grammatical and polished if you hope to project a professional image of yourself and your company.

Perhaps the greatest conversational evil is in using inappropriate *subject-verb combinations:* For instance, "He don't think he gonna ... be there on time," is not an acceptable way of saying "He doesn't think he'll be there on time."

I recognize that many readers may be so aware of grammatical rules that I may be running a risk of insulting them, and I apologize. Please make sure that your telemarketers speak proper English, and if they do not, encourage them to sign up for English and Speech classes, with emphasis upon the former category.

In a later section I'll discuss regional speech habits and point out that you can establish a certain amount of rapport by adopting, at least temporarily, various local phrases. Please don't confuse these comments with what I have said above. You need to learn the rules before you can selectively overrule them.

Winners don't suffer from these five problems. They also do a number of things that promote rapport quickly.

The Great Secret to Being Liked
That No One May Have Shared With You

There is a secret to causing others to like you. It is so simple that when I first heard it I said, "Aw, come on ..."

Here is the secret to "making" others like you: Like them first.

I knew that back in kindergarten, didn't you? Of course you did. But we forgot it somewhere on the way to becoming sophisticated adults.

As a matter of fact it was a very learned psychologist who reminded me of this little gem. Think about if for a moment.

Who do you like? Why do you think you like them? If you discount all of the presumed reasons we affiliate with others such as attitude similarity, sharing the same place of employment, and living in the same neighborhood, I assure you that you'll be able to see one thing that unites all of the people that you like: They like you, too.

Of course, they show very good taste in doing so, we all know that! But seriously, if you want to create rapport with others on the phone, you need to send them a signal that you like them. And you can't wait until it is "safe," when they have done likewise for you. You have to take a small risk and show a sign of admiration or appreciation at the very beginning of the call.

How can you do it? One way is through your voice.

I had a professor in graduate school who was probably one of the best mentors to his students of any member of the faculty. Some professors in Ph.D. programs teach through intimidation and fear in an effort to shock students into working hard and producing original work.

Not this individual. He always showed respect toward his students, making us feel that we possessed the kind of gift that could make a difference in the world. His attitude came through in his communication style. When we would make comments he would lean forward in his chair and encourage us as we spoke with the words, "Yes ...yes ... I see ...," and so forth.

It made you feel terrific. I can only describe his tone as

containing a certain amount of optimism, interest, and focus. As a matter of fact, it was also very, very *friendly*.

I can't underestimate the power of this sort of tone. It may be *the* most essential quality in interpersonal communication, because it makes a person feel important as well as liked.

Show Interest in Them Right Away

Ask people how they are when you begin a conversation. This promotes the call in a number of ways: First, it enables you to draw the person into the conversation and create a sense of shared ownership of the transaction. The prospect is involved quickly, therefore developing a stake in the successful outcome of the call.

Second, by asking the person how he or she is you are able to put the call on a personal level without running a very high risk of seeming presumptuous.

It is true that some people aren't too fond of being asked about their mood at the beginning of a call, particularly by a stranger. For them, this kind of inquiry can sound insincere because they claim that a stranger isn't really interested in them to begin with.

Fortunately, the people who dislike the effort are in the minority. Most people perceive your question as a courtesy. It shows interest, and it tells the prospect that he or she is important.

Don't Scare Them with Too Much Seriousness

Many telemarketers are weakened by something I labeled as phone fear some time ago (see *Winning by Telephone*, Prentice-Hall, 1982, and *Reach Out & Sell Someone*, Prentice-Hall, 1983). Phone fear is also known as call reluctance. It is the telephonic equivalent of stage fright.

Phone fear is simply being afraid that you are going to sound foolish or dumb to the person on the other end of the phone. This fear causes you to procrastinate and make various compensations for it in your selling style. I knew one fellow about fifteen years ago who used to stand on top of his desk with phone in hand, nearly shouting into the receiver at his prospects. This technique made him feel superior to the potential client and enabled him to "get down" to the business of selling.

This is an extreme example, I grant you, but folks with phone fear will do other things that will inhibit the creation of customer rapport. When you are afraid, you often overcompensate by trying to sound totally unemotional and smooth. Don't try to sound stuffy or overly serious. You'll only induce defensiveness in the customer.

A Certain Down-Home Quality Can Help

I know one telemarketer who claims that his most effective phone manner is what he calls "My Good-Ole-Boy-Act." He comes from the Carolinas, so he feels comfortable using his native tones while communicating with potential customers. He claims extraordinary results as well. If you ask, he'll tell you that he tries to keep things extremely simple and on the humble side. He makes sure to downplay the fact that he possesses a Phi Beta Kappa key when he presents himself as being "just plain folks."

Adjust Your Friendliness to Various Regions

I hate to say it, but it can be really dumb to sound too eager and friendly when speaking with hard-bitten Easterners. Don't get me wrong, I have a lot of friends on the East Coast, but they didn't become my friends until we had passed through certain rituals or communication exchanges that occurred over time.

It's a different matter when dealing with many Southerners. There is a much greater emphasis placed upon hospitality there, something which is carried over into telephone conversations. In fact, when I consult for national clients where I travel across the country and train salespeople in various offices, I find that some issues and challenges that are pertinent to Northerners aren't really as important to their Southern counterparts.

For instance, it seems a lot easier for a field salesperson to "invite him- or herself" to a prospect's office for a visit in Atlanta or

Birmingham than it is in Hartford or Philadelphia. Similarly, managing conversations with secretaries seems to be a warmer process in the Southern climes.

In any case, you can luxuriate in spending more time establishing rapport in Southern and Western states than you can in Midwestern and Eastern ones. Adjust your presentations accordingly.

Monitor How You Are Doing from Time to Time

The most effective telemarketers develop a sixth sense for how their calls are proceeding. This comes from attending to certain details during the conversation. The only way you can be sensitive to these details is through what I call intensive listening: As you may have guessed, ordinary listening is inadequate for our purposes as most of us miss too many valuable verbal cues when we listen in the normal manner. Ordinary listening is substantially easier than the telephonic kind because you are usually in the speaker's presence, and if you miss something your lack of response will trigger the speaker to repeat what you have missed. In addition, when you are looking at someone you can read the person's lips if his or her articulation makes normal decoding of the message difficult.

Telephone listening needs to be acute, accurate, and extremely fast. Here is what you should tune in for:

The customer's mood:
- How does the customer answer the phone?
  - Quickly? Slowly?
- Does it sound like you have interrupted?
- Is his or her voice rushed or relaxed?
- Is his or her tone upbeat or downcast?

The customer's language:
- Polite or blunt?
- Keyed into your greeting or coming at you from "left field?"
- Are the words spontaneously chosen or very carefully selected?

Background noises:
- Can you hear the customer breathing?
- Are there distracting noises in the background? Other voices? Loud machinery?

The customer's dialect:
- Where does it sound like the person is from, originally:
  - The East?
  - The Midwest?
  - The South?
  - The West?

The momentum of the call:
- As with many things, conversations tend to go forward or backward, or to stall. Where is this one headed?

I am the first to admit that these are lots of details that I am asking you to be conscious of and to monitor. Much of your success in the first ten seconds will depend upon the cultivation and use of your sharpened listening skills.

Here are some of the reasons these particular items are worth noting:

Customer Mood

The speed with which the phone is answered gives you an idea as to how busy the person is. If it is answered immediately, you can assume that he or she is ready to concentrate on your message. If it takes a long time to reach a given person, you may have caught the person at an inopportune moment. Don't assume that this is the case and ask if it is okay to address the person. You may inadvertently implant the idea yourself, resulting in a premature termination of the contact.

If the person seems out of breath or particularly agitated, it may then be appropriate to volunteer a comment such as "It sounds like I have reached you at a busy time; am I right?" If they affirm this, then say, without first hearing an invitation, "Well, I'll call you back later, okay?" This allows you to maintain control of the conversation while creating an obligation on the part of the prospect to attempt to be available when you do call again.

We often misjudge people's voices in respect to the attitudes they are conveying. If we feel defensive after having heard put-downs from prospect after prospect it's likely that we'll be psychologically predisposed toward hearing boos instead of applause when we venture our next call.

Remember an important point in telemarketing: Many people sound "cold" over the phone without knowing it. Don't jump to the conclusion that they don't like you if they fail to sound "warm and tingly" right away. Give them a chance before making a definite judgment.

Customer Language

If a customer sounds overly blunt with you at the beginning of a call, you should be prepared to abbreviate your talk by engineering an agreement to continue.

Let's say a customer wants to get off the line and this is why he or she is coming across as being overly blunt. Stop where you are and ask what I call a "bottom-line qualifying question." Interrupt yourself with the words "Just a quick question, Mr./Ms. Frisbee." This will help you to stay in control. Than add your question. "If we can show you how to save money through a minimal outlay, this will be something you'll want to pursue; am I right?" If he or she really has heartburn with you, your product or your firm, the bait will be refused. Otherwise, an affirmation that saving money would be worth pursuing will give your phone call a new life.

If you hear a prospect using extremely guarded language, it is safe to assume that the person is not a friend of the sales process. Try to loosen her lips by asking if there is anything else that you may not have taken into account. This is the "brother-in-law question," which is geared to determining if some relative has the inside track on being awarded the business or if there are any unknown factors that you may be bucking that will spell disaster for your efforts.

If you don't reap more information through this type of ploy, either find another champion in the firm to help you or select another prospect entirely.

Background Noises

When you are speaking to a prospect and you hear a number of other speakers in the background who are on telephones themselves, this can be a clue that the person you are speaking to has either the busiest office in the world or not much status and clout.

In a similar vein, if a person has placed you on a speakerphone, chances are good that you are making your presentation to more than one person. If this bothers you, you can politely mention that the connection is weak and ask the prospect to pick up his or her telephone receiver and speak directly into it.

Customer's Dialect

If you detect a dialect in the customer's voice, you may have made a very opportune discovery. This may provide you with a great chance to create psychological identification with the person by shaping your voice to match his or hers. I have called this process "code switching" or "voice blending," and it is one of the quickest methods of creating rapport available to you at the beginning of a call (for a complete discussion, refer to *Reach Out & Sell Someone*, Prentice-Hall, 1983).

Each of us possesses three vocal nuances; rate, melody, and volume. These three comprise our *vocal signature*, which, on the one hand, gives us a unique sound, and on the other it ties us to a larger group of people who sound like we do: For instance, some data processing professionals sound very much like engineers and air traffic controllers. All of their voices tend to border on a monotone. They sound very matter-of-fact, and there is less emotion conveyed in their voices than in the voices of people who are involved in sales and customer service work.

DP professionals, engineers, and air traffic controllers' voices can be described as having:

- A somewhat slow and lumbering *rate*.
- Little *melodic* variation as they move from idea to idea.
- A low-key level of *volume*. These people tend not to shout.

What you should do is identify a person's vocal signature as quickly as you can, which means that you should get a "fix" on it during their response to your greeting. If the person comes through a certain way, don't fight it; instead, go along with it, and try unobtrusively to match what you are hearing. You'll find you get along with all kinds of people.

Momentum

You'll know that you have momentum in a call when a customer starts giving you what are called "therapeutic grunts." These are the little utterances of feedback that are volunteered by a listener who is tracking what you are saying, and who is himself telling us, "You're okay so far."

Therapeutic grunts are phrases such as "uh-huh," "yeah," "okay," and "all right." You'll know them when you hear them.

When you have established rapport, you'll be ready for your next 10-second challenge—establishing your credibility—which we'll explore in Chapter 3.

The first 10 seconds in review:
1. Listen to your voice on tape and determine how you sound to prospects.
2. Don't worry about "not sounding a certain way." Build a positive plan for your delivery.
3. Sound like a winner by:

   • Sounding positive.
   • Articulating properly.
   • Carrying the conversation yourself.
   • Sounding mature.
   • Using standard English.

4. To make others like you, *like them first.*
5. Show interest in the prospect by asking how he or she is.
6. Don't sound overly serious.
7. Try to sound neighborly.
8. Adjust your friendliness to different regions.
9. Monitor how you come across through *intensive listening.*

10. Be sensitive to the:

   - Customer's mood.
   - Customer's language.
   - Background noises.
   - Customer's dialect.
   - Momentum of the call.

11. Identify the customer's *vocal signature* and match it.

The Second 10 Seconds
Positioning and Credibility

I am going to mention a series of products that are advertised on television, and I want you to take a little quiz for me, okay?

Here's how it works: After you hear the name of the product, write down the name of the person who appears in the ads hustling each product.

Here we go:

1. Polaroid. *Garner* *malden*
2. American Express.
3. Paul Masson Wines.
4. Xerox. *Klugman*
5. Sanka.
6. Pepsi. *clabs*
7. Lite Beer. *groups* *sports*
8. Sears Financial Network.
9. Alpo. *Loren Green*
10. Chrysler. *Iacocca*

How many were you able to come up with right away? Four? Five? All of them?

Some are pretty easy, aren't they? Karl Malden for American Express, James Garner for Polaroid, and Hal Holbrook for Sears probably came to you right off the bat.

Have you ever asked yourself what Karl Malden knows about credit cards? Probably no more than we do. And I'll bet James Garner is no Ansel Adams when it comes to photography; speaking of which, how many common people have heard of Ansel Adams, the famous photographic artist whose works on the High Sierra have been inspirational to backpackers and naturalists for decades?

Not nearly as many as have heard of James Garner, that's for sure. Maybe Polaroid knew what it was doing when it selected the latter to be its spokesperson instead of the former.

Come to think of it, what does Hal Holbrook know about investments? I'll bet my last T-Bill that he's ignorant of the really savvy strategies involved in the financial world, but he does know something about playing Abraham Lincoln in a one-man show that was seen by millions. Lincoln was honest, and I guess Holbrook must be honest and trustworthy too, and I therefore might conclude that Sears is a solid place to put my money.

If this reasoning sounds a little strained and indirect, it is. But it is precisely these sorts of considerations that inform the thinking of advertising agencies when they deliberate upon hiring a spokesperson to represent and be the "mouthpiece" for various products and services.

Ad agencies are betting on a number of assumptions when they select a known personality or celebrity to tout a given product:

1. It takes credibility to sell something.
2. Credibility can be earned through various avenues.

Why are ex-athletes hot properties on the lecture circuit? What does being the quarterback of a football team have to do with running a multimillion-dollar organization? Leadership? Sure. Motivational prowess? Certainly. Being able to run the hundred in less than nine flat?

No way. The comparisons stop at this point between athletes and executives, I think. Nonetheless, *people tend to believe that someone who is credible in one domain may be credible in another.*

Why do "stars" who play medical doctors in the soaps find themselves accosted in supermarkets and begged for prescriptions for various maladies from which fellow shoppers and loyal TV fans suffer? Many of these poor actors haven't seen a college, let alone a medical school.

But they seem so *believable!* This is the quality that advertisers and sponsors are buying, and it is the same quality that you need to convey over the phone to be successful with your prospects.

Believability: What Is It?

When I ask seminar groups to enumerate the qualities that successful salespeople possess, *sincerity* always pops up. The next question gets tougher: What *is* sincerity?

Honesty. Truthfulness. Integrity. Caring. Okay, I'll buy these descriptions, but how do you convey these qualities through telephone lines when you can't be seen and the firmness of your handshake can't be assessed?

Again, you have two basic tools for expressing anything over the phone: words and voice. Through the clever modulation of these elements you can become believable, and after you do, sales will start to roll in.

People Crave Authority

Do you remember asking your parents why you couldn't go out and play and they said: "Because I said so!"?

What power! It takes a great authority to provide an explanation such as this which really isn't an explanation at all.

When we borrow a little bit of the "parent voice" at the beginning of the conversation we are asserting "rights" over the call that are nearly irresistible to the listener. We are tapping into a dusty old psychological program that the prospect has been carrying around into adulthood. It's akin to sending a signal to a receiver that has been tuned to a certain channel, but has not heard any tranmissions for several years. The receiver still works, and there is no reason not to employ it in our sales efforts.

I'll give you an example. Most telemarketers have to deal with screeners, or folks who function as gatekeepers, thus determining who will pass through the telephonic entrance to the company and who will be left in the cold. Normally, salespeople grow upset with these functionaries because they are made to feel powerless, as children doubtless feel from time to time.

"May I ask who's calling?"

"Does he know you?"

"Is he expecting your call?"

"Are you *selling* something?"

Many of these questions can feel demeaning, and salespeople tend to recoil upon hearing them. Moreover, sellers become angry that they are being so poorly treated, and they start expressing their anger to the screener, which only makes the latter redouble his or her efforts.

What I suggest is that we turn the tables upon the screener. Sound like you are *their* parents in the same way that they have exerted power over you by sounding like yours!

This is accomplished through both voice and words. Your tone needs to be saying:

"Look, don't mess with me: I've called this joint before, and I'm *not* impressed, okay?"

I suggest you change "the screening ritual," as I have called it, to reflect *your* agenda for the call.

For instance, most of us position ourselves rather poorly by asking:

"Is Bill Smith in?"

Right away, the screener is tipped off that you are a small fry and not a heavyweight. Timid people ask questions such as this, while powerful people announce who they are before requesting anything.

Here's how I announce myself:

"Hello, Dr. Goodman for Bill Smith; thank you!"

This sort of statement tells the listener who you are, who you wish to speak to, while thanking the person in advance for his or her assistance. It accomplishes these things in one conversational statement, while saving everyone's time and energy.

For a complete discussion of how to negotiate the screening process, I suggest you look into my book, *You Can Sell Anything by Telephone!* (Prentice-Hall, 1984). In the meantime, remember that a good deal of your positioning will occur in how you come across to the screener as well as the prospect, and there is no better way to sound than a little bit like an impatient parent.

Obedience Comes Naturally

Stanley Milgram of Yale conducted some revealing studies on the subject of obedience a number of years ago. These experiments were the subject of a special dramatic television program starring William Shatner .ome time later.

Milgram established that "normal" people possessed an extraordinary capability of obeying commands from their superiors and from figures of authority. The experiments were designed as "learning experiences," in which subjects were instructed to act as "teachers" and administer increasing levels of electrical shock to "students" who missed answers on tests.

What the "teachers" weren't told was the fact that the experiments were rigged and that, in reality, they weren't causing discomfort to the pupils, even though the pupils would scream as the bogus shock was being administered.

Occasionally, those who were asked to play the role of teacher found it uncomfortable and questioned whether the pupils really "had to" be punished through electric shocks. The people who appeared to be in charge of the experiments, who were dressed in white laboratory coats, simply replied, "The experiment must continue."

As the shocks were administered, a control panel indicated the severity of the jolt that was occurring at the time. A number of "teachers" went to the end of the scale into the highest zone, and as they did, the screams that they were hearing turned into ominous silences.

It sounds like science fiction, doesn't it? It isn't, though.

These experiments and others like them have demonstrated that there exists in people a veritable appetite for responding to authority, and history provides several stark examples of times when this motive has gone haywire, resulting in massive devastation.

The positive feature of this phenomenon lies in the fact that we can position ourselves as authorities and create consent and rather deep psychological commitment in a very brief telephone exchange.

Assumptive People Make Opportunities Where None Existed Before

My company was doing some consulting work for a client in the New York area a few months ago and three of us went into a wonderful little Italian restaurant for dinner. This wasn't just any old restaurant, as the decor informed us as we walked in.

Instead of providing the standard fare of tables and chairs, this restaurant offered tables, yes, but couches in which to sit. And they weren't just plain old couches, either. They were salmon-colored *velour* couches.

We were struck by the fact that this was the kind of place that would require reservations, which of course, none of us had had the foresight to make. It was no help that the place seemed pretty jammed, and only one table appeared to be available as I approached the maitre d'.

Here is how I positioned my party:

"Dr. Goodman, party of three; thank you."

Notice any similarity in this statement when you think back to how I said I introduce my telephone calls? Right you are! It's practically the same message.

Here's what happened next. The tuxedoed gentleman turned to me with tremendous Old World composure and asked:

"Do you have a reservation?"

I replied, "No!"

The next thing that happened was truly magical. The head tuxedo turned to the second-string tuxedo and said in a beautiful voice, "Please show Dr. Goodman's party to table eleven." That's right, we were whisked off to the only available table in the place. Before moving in that direction I glanced at the reservation sheet and I saw a number of parties whose names were on the list. "Whatever became of them," I wondered.

You're probably asking what was so incredible about my performance. I'll tell you. It was all in the way I said "No!"

Remember one principle: In most interpersonal encounters the law of the jungle is slightly modified to reflect our civility. It isn't "kill or be killed," but "intimidate or be intimidated."

New York restaurateurs are no bozos when it comes to knowing how to create a haughty climate and intimidate customers. In fact, it can even be argued that customers are willing to pay more for the "privilege" of being abused by personnel in first-class restaurants because it reinforces the image of exclusivity that many establishments promote.

Why did this maitre d' become so cooperative? I said "no" with the following inflection in my voice:

"Are you kidding? *Me* make reservations in a dump like this? You can't be serious! Do you have any idea of the stature of the person with whom you are speaking?"

Get the idea? I intimidated his socks off and positioned our party right into some very, very scarce space—the only remaining table in the house.

If you had asked this maitre d' if he would be giving away his only table to someone who didn't have a reservation he would have asked if you were crazy. The assumptive quality of my message to him actually created an opportunity where none had existed before.

There is no Other Alternative in This Situation

To sound assumptive you need to convey a sense of irresistable purpose, seriousness, and "inevitability." Here's what I mean: People will follow a leader, and a leader is someone who seems to know where he or she is headed most of the time. Leaders also seemed to be "wired into" destiny. General Patton believed he had been reincarnated several times and thought he had served in battle throughout the ages. Much of his sense of assumptiveness seemed to spring from his conviction that history would not deny him great successes.

For Patton, there was no alternative but greatness and drama in the theaters of war. When we are at our best on the phone we embody the same sense of *inevitability*.

Of course we're going to earn this sale! Yes, Mr./Ms. Customer, you are going to want to buy! Who wouldn't want to if they were in your position?

If You Want Respect You Need to Be a Little Larger Than Life

When it comes to customers, everyone is a Texan: they like to be dealing with *BIG* things. I am continually amazed at this habit of dealing "with the biggest" as it is manifested in ordinary business deals.

What is IBM's corporate nickname? "Big Blue," of course, and you might be amazed at the reverence in people's voices when they utter this alternative name for the corporate giant. A part of the reason people are attracted to bigness resides in the very American notion that "Bigger is better."

"Small is beautiful" was a sweet and successful Volkswagen advertising appeal in the 1960s, but it never really caught on with the great mass of Americans. We may have traded in our automotive "fins" several fuel crunches ago, but V-8's are starting to roar off assembly lines as fast as you can say "turbocharge it!"

Bigness can be communicated in various ways during the

second ten seconds of your call. Look at the way you announce the specifics about what your company does:

> "Hello, Mr./Ms. Frisbee? This is Gary Goodman with Goodman Communications. How are things with you today?
>
> "Well, fine. Our company is in the telemarketing training business, and ..."

This is just about the way most folks describe their firms and, as you can tell, it leaves a lot to be desired.

"We're in the telemarketing training business" can not only be called a dull statement, but it arouses a feeling of "So what?" in the customer. Moreover, a lackluster description such as this one can actually set up customer resistance by making my firm seem to be a "me-too" entity, which of course, is far from the truth.

In short, there is nothing in my utterance at this point that tells the client we are *big enough* to warrant his further attention, and there is a certain amount of negative momentum or "call lag" that begins to retard the sales process.

The customer is probably thinking, "I'm not going to get anything positive out of this call." This is a point in the conversation when the prospect should be made to feel that there are many good reasons for continuing the coversation. In other words, he or she should be thinking, "This call could be very fruitful for me."

Now, how do you make this sort of perception occur, instead? Let's begin by rewriting your statement about the company:

> "Well, fine. Goodman Communications is regarded as the leader in telemarketing training, and ..."

Does this sound like a little bit of puffery? In a way it may be, but you truly believe you're the best, so it makes sense to let others in on the secret in order that they may take advantage of your prowess, right? In other words, if you don't sound sold on the credibility of your firm, how are you going to convince anybody else?

Note that I repeated the name of my firm, Goodman Communications. This lets the name reverberate again in the prospect's consciousness, while making the unspoken claim that this name is worth repeating. It also creates a bit of aesthetic distance between the speaker and the corporate identity. By saying Goodman Communications does such and such, the speaker can attribute greater successes to this entity than if he said "we" do such and such extremely well. In saying "we're great," you can turn listeners off faster than if you seem to be speaking of a company identity without the personal ownership suggested in the egoistic pronoun, "we."

I followed the company name with the words, "... is regarded as the leader in telemarketing training, and ..."

By whom are we regarded as the leaders in telemarketing training? We don't attribute this reference to anyone, which encourages the listener to infer that we are considered experts by people who are in a position to judge such distinctions.

I am communicating the "bigness" of Goodman Communications through this initial announcement of identity, and from this point forward I should have achieved the focused attention of the prospect. Additionally, he or she should be perceiving me as a credible source at this time and feel comfortable in investing a more substantial period with me in conversation.

And Now, the Reason for Your Call ...

Why are you on the phone at this moment? For the listener to continue with you in comfort, you need to address this question right away.

This portion of the second ten seconds creates your legitimacy. There are several reasons for your call, which I have discussed at length elsewhere (see *Reach Out & Sell Someone*, Prentice-Hall, 1983).

In brief, here are some of your justifications:

1. *You are following up a letter or brochure.* This is a tremendous source of credibility and legitimacy for prospects. When you make reference to mailers that they have or haven't seen, you are perceived as more "real" than you would appear if you were only a disembodied voice coming through the telephone.

2. *You are preceding a mailing with a call.* This is also a good gambit because it seems somewhat formal in a good way. Here, you are taking the pains to announce a forthcoming mailer; and in so doing, you are creating a commitment on the part of the prospects to give it a thorough reading. Who knows, you may call again to quiz them on its contents!

3. *You are following up advertising in the media.* Advertising can also be referred to with a positive effect, in the fashion as the mailers we referred to above. You can also get a reading on the effectiveness and recall value of various ads that you place through this device.

4. *You are following up a referral from a friend or acquaintance.* Referral selling is an established procedure. When prospects hear that we have been recommended by a credible third party, we are in a very good position to influence the buyer.

5. *You are announcing a new product or service.* Prospects perk up their ears when they hear the word "new," and this can provide you with the right amount of interest to fuel your sales talk.

6. *You are performing a survey or doing market research.* Research is a worthy enterprise and listeners are often quite cooperative in answering questions when it seems that it is for a reasonable cause.

You should take care in ensuring that the listener doesn't come to feel that this is your *exclusive* reason for calling, for when it comes to light that you are selling, some disappointment and resentment can occur.

7. *You are inviting the prospect to participate in a special occasion.* Many organizations use seminars as a way of acquainting prospects with products and services. Seminars can be attractive, inasmuch as they usually contain a substantial educational payoff for attendees and various components, such as well respected speakers, free meals, and the like, can appear especially attractive.

8. *You have developed a useful idea for the prospect.* I'll often be glancing through newspapers and magazines and light upon an idea that seems to stimulate an idea that one of my prospects or clients can use.

By mentioning this fact early in a telephone call I can generate interest and convey a certain amount of concern and enthusiasm for his or her organization.

9. *You are calling to thank a customer for something he or she did for you in the past.* This sort of conversational prelude can work wonders for the reception you receive from buyers.

Unfortunately, few people are told how important and appreciated they are. If you take a minute for this purpose, it can literally make their day.

10. *You are saying hello to an inactive account.* In most industrial situations, the file cabinets and customer data systems contain potential "gold" for telemarketers that usually remains untapped.

In reality, customers who have been overlooked for months, and in some cases even years, are usually very pleased to hear from you. They may have found new vendors who weren't nearly as competent as your company's, yet they may have been embarrassed to make the first move by getting in touch with you.

As I mentioned, these openers are discussed in detail in Chapter 4 of *Reach Out & Sell Someone* (Prentice-Hall, 1983). When you use them you'll find that you present the call in an interesting and dignified way that encourages the customer to maintain his commitment to the conversation.

Customers Need to Participate Early in the Call

People have asked me for years why folks who call them at home tend to be so unprofessional and obnoxious. There are a few reasons: Typical telephone "solicitors" receive little or no training. They seem to be uninvolved with what they are doing, and one gets the feeling that their true mission in life has little to do with the purpose of their phone calls to us.

Accordingly, the scripts they use are terribly one-sided. It seems that they do all the talking, while the prospect is required to tolerate an amateurish message until the caller decides it is time for the listener to assent to the bargain.

Professional telemarketing, to be credible with the corporate buyer and the sophisticated consumer, must be built upon a foundation of *mutuality*. No one party can afford to dominate, or at least seem to control, the conversation through transparent and obtrusive strategies.

This means that the customer should once again be consulted during the second ten seconds, as he or she was during the first, when you asked how he or she was after announcing who you were.

This second effort at involving the customer can take many forms:

1. *You can ask a direct question.* This can be a simple request for factual data; an example of this is validating the accuracy of a mailing address that you have for the customer.
2. *You can ask a qualifying question.* This is an excellent way of determining the seriousness of the potential buyer, and his or her ability to afford what you are selling.

    An accepted type of qualifying question is phrased in an "if-then" fashion:

    "If we can show you how to save on your income taxes next year, and do this inexpensively, this is probably something you will want to pursue further; am I right?

3. *You can ask a rhetorical question.* This type of question is one where you don't really hope for a full-fledged answer, but rather an "affirmative grunt," which tells you that you are pursuing the right approach with the customer at that point during the call.

    A rhetorical question can be phrased as follows:

    "Have you ever thought how wonderful it would be to save a little more money on taxes next year?"

    If you wish even less client participation in the call at this time, you can turn this question into more of a statement that you hope will be affirmed by the listener:

"I'll bet you've probably thought that it would be nice to save a little bit on your taxes next year ..."

4. *You can use various "you" statements.* This is an easy way of creating a sense of customer involvement throughout the call. As you know, it's very important to get involved with a message. I'm sure you've often felt that a salesperson was in a presentation only for him or herself; am I right?

Well, as you may have detected, I did the very thing I am advocating in the last three sentences, including this one you are reading right now! Each of the previous three sentences contained references to "you." This pronoun creates almost instantaneous satisfaction in the listener because he or she thinks you are addressing him or her as an individual.

"You" statements are also very helpful in dealing with problem listeners, as I have pointed out in *Winning by Telephone* (Prentice-Hall, 1982).

All of the devices mentioned in this chapter will assist you in presenting your message and building your credibility at the same time. After reviewing this chapter's tips, we'll move into The Third Ten Seconds: Discussing Your Products and Services.

The second 10 seconds in review:

1. Remember that it takes credibility to sell something, and credibility can be earned in various ways.
2. To be perceived as credible, you need to seem sincere and believable.
3. Remember: People crave authority; you can create positive responses by sounding responsible, occasionally "parent-like," and assumptive.
4. Assumptive people make opportunities where none existed before.
5. Learn to convey a sense of irresistible purpose, seriousness, and "inevitability."
6. People respect "bigness," and it is wise to position your firm as one of the strongest and the best.
7. Use a specific reason for making the call that will put the customer at ease and encourage him or her to listen to more of your message.
8. Encourage customers to participate in the second ten seconds of the call, although you will be controlling their level of involvement.

4

The Third 10 Seconds

Describing Your Products and Services

We've all heard the expression, "Build a better mousetrap and the world will beat a path to your door." If we were to update this verity, it might read; "Genetically engineer a microorganism that will cause sexual confusion in otherwise fertile rats, and then offer stock to the public; you will become very rich."

In any case, the idea that is advanced by these statements is that riches will automatically come to the person or people who make a needed or improved product. Unfortunately, this reasoning is suspect. No one will bestow great fortunes upon you for creating pet rocks and other fantastic products unless you strategically convince them that your efforts will be beneficial.

Speaking of pet rocks, *that* was a classic example of a victory of hype over functionality. In the pet rock "phenomenon" we saw an entrepreneur who cannily satirized two sacred American institutions at once: household pets and modern merchandising. The lesson in the pet rock fad lies in recognizing that people only need "good reasons" for buying anything, and these can be either extremely farfetched or very "reasonable," depending on the point of view of the person judging the transaction.

In this chapter we're going to take a very close look at your options in making your products and services sound most attractive to buyers during the third ten seconds of your presentation.

Classic Errors in Describing Products and Services

Before pointing out some of the best approaches to the product-description process, let's look at some of the classic errors that sellers make.

1. *They take too much time "popping off."* Remember that telephone listeners have very limited attention spans. I have reported elsewhere that the estimated average adult attention span is four seconds long during face-to-face interactions, which are rich in visual dynamics (see *Winning by Telephone*, Prentice-Hall, 1982). You can only imagine how frequently prospects tune out during phone calls!

This problem makes it important for you to keep your product descriptions short and to the point. When you become long-winded, buyers become distracted.

2. *They get overly technical.* It seems that phone calls weren't made for dealing with overly technical descriptions. This applies especially to those calls where you haven't had any past dealings with the buyer.

People gravitate toward simplicity, anyway. Think about typical American folk heroes. Will Rogers and Mark Twain come to my mind immediately. These fellows both had the gift of telling stories that appeared to be terribly simple, yet which owed their impact to *irony*, which is very subtle and requires near-genius to develop properly.

Just as Twain and Rogers told very "simple" stories with "a twist," you as a salesperson need to come through in the same sort of down-to-earth manner, although you may be dealing with pretty complex issues.

3. *They can assume too much knowledge or interest.* My company was performing a telemarketing campaign recently where we were calling manufacturers and announcing forthcoming seminars. The presentation we were using was really tight and sounded very smooth, and our callers were in top form.

There was only one problem, though. Most of the people we spoke to confessed that they were mystified by the term "tele-marketing," which appeared several times during the talk. This was curious to us, because we were operating on the assumption that some 93 percent of industrial firms were using telemarketing. While this may have been true, the fact remained that a large number of companies that we contacted had never associated what they were doing with this particular term.

This sort of experience reminds you that you cannot assume that your prospects possess more sophistication than they do. We were lucky. Early in our calling efforts we were effectively warned by our customers that we needed to translate our jargon into terms that they could appreciate.

4. *They can sound overly laudatory.* It's wonderful to be proud of your products while having the enthusiasm to share your feelings with customers. It is a mistake, however, to praise your wares beyond credulity and reasonableness.

Some salespeople can't resist making outrageous claims, it seems. They belong in that bygone era of medicine shows, where all-purpose cure-alls were touted before gullible audiences.

These days all salespeople are confronted with what researchers have labeled, "the obstinate audience," or people who respond to sellers with strong disbelief, which becomes belief only after it has been dispelled with a certain amount of logic and the right amount of puffery about the products and services in question.

5. *They can damn their products with faint praise.* Just as you can be guilty of exaggerating the value of your wares, you can commit the opposite error as well.

Veteran salespeople can fall into this trap when they don't want to sound like salespeople so they consciously "undersell" the client.

Several weeks ago, I spoke to a moderately successful insurance agent who belonged to this group of people. "Look," he said, "if you want coverage, you'll have to call me, because I'm not going to chase you or persuade you to do anything." This may sound like a kindly gesture on his part, but he's really copping out when it comes to alerting me about the value of his coverage versus that of other agents.

In his line of work, underselling could prove tragic if someone failed to protect his or her family with sufficient coverage because the agent wanted to avoid the stigma of seeming to come across as a salesperson.

When it comes to underselling, I look at it this way: "If I don't tell the client how good we are, who will?"

What You're Selling Isn't Necessarily What the Customer Is Buying!

Cadillac built its first "Cimmaron" model a few years ago, and it suffered a major disappointment as it witnessed sluggish sales and a general rejection in the marketplace. How did this first-rate division of General Motors make such a mistake?

Cadillac recognized for some time a trend toward: (1) Downsized cars which offered substantial fuel economy, and (2) increasing American purchases of foreign cars—particularly those of Mercedes-Benz, BMW, and Volvo.

To address these circumstances, Cadillac built a small car that was very plain on the exterior, while offering some of the sumptuous amenities it had been known to build into larger models. Cadillac erred in allowing other General Motors divisions to use the same basic body style for cheaper imitations of their own. This confused the buyer and retarded sales.

I believe Cadillac failed to read the signals in the marketplace that were around during the inception of the Cimmaron. First, American luxury car buyers were tired of the hefty depreciation that U.S. cars were subject to because of numerous body styling changes. European manufacturers tended to retain certain styles for substantially longer periods of time than we did. Moreover, Americans came to associate luxury not with superficial appointments such as leather interiors and electric seats, but rather with status, exclusivity, and that which appears "chic."

Cadillac wasn't competing on familiar ground. Its image was more closely associated with cigar-smoking "fat cats" than with lithe and nimble joggers and health nuts who wanted their cars to be muscular and elegant without having the softness and decadent pudginess associated with the old-fashioned "couches on wheels," that American luxury cruisers had come to represent.

In short, the Cadillac lifestyle was at odds in a fundamental way with how younger, affluent Americans were viewing themselves, and it was these people who would constitute a market for a smaller car from that firm.

I have to believe that U.S. auto executives failed to read the foreign challenge at least in part because they were amazed that "people could be so dumb" as to spend a lot of money on tiny, uncomfortable European and Japanese vehicles. To auto bigwigs, such consumer behavior must have seemed like a passing fad that would correct itself if ignored.

Perhaps the biggest blow to Cadillac's ego came when it recognized that Cadillac itself was no longer the "Cadillac of the industry"—Mercedes-Benz had replaced it, if only unofficially.

I understand that Cadillac plans to reposition itself in the marketplace by offering cars that have price tags in the neighborhood of $150,000 and up. It seems this manufacturer is recognizing that having a Cadillac isn't much fun anymore when "nearly anyone" can afford one.

The moral to the Cimarron story is this: *Customers see benefits in products that many of us would never predict; and, at the same time, customers are known to completely ignore aspects of products that we, the sellers, believe are essential to any prospect's well-being.* The key to succeeding with customers is in pointing out the right advantages to owning or using your wares.

What Makes a Product or Service Attractive?

People make buying decisions based upon several factors, although some of us would like to believe that most people use logic alone. Here are some of the motivations to buy:

Fears

Recently, the brakes on one of my cars started to fade. In fact, fade isn't the right word. "Disappear" would be more accurate.

I'd come to a traffic signal and place my foot on the pedal, and my foot would start to sink to the floorboard, while the car would begin to roll forward.

I'll bet you can guess what thought coursed through my mind when this process took place for the second or third time.

"I'd better trade this lemon in" was the notion that shot through my consciousness like a comet.

I was responding to a very potent form of motivation: fear. I'm not alone in my concern for my life, and insurance underwriters and other businesspeople who use fear appeals in selling are well aware of this fact.

Fear can work effectively in a telephone appeal if you are prudent in its use. There is a body of literature in the behavioral sciences that addresses the issue of how much fear is to be used in persuasion. If too much fear is aroused, you can force the prospect to reject the message if you aren't careful.

Cognitive Consistency

Do you do your grocery shopping in the same store week after week? If you are like me, the answer is probably yes.

Why do we keep going to the same stores when we might find better bargains and service at some other locale? Habit is one reason. We are indeed creatures of habit, and we tend to repeat past behaviors because we associate them with safety or success.

Another reason we do the same things over and again is found in something called "cognitive consistency." Some psychologists claim that we have a fundamental need for maintaining psychological harmony, or balance, as it is termed, and one of the surest methods of accomplishing this is to repeat past behaviors while coming to see our actions as internally logical and consistent.

By telling prospects that your products or services "fit in" with their publicly proclaimed plans or past actions, you are appealing to the need for cognitive consistency.

I can't tell you how many times I have heard prospects say that they were hesitant about buying because "We've never done anything like this before!" It is your task as a persuader to create rhetorically the feeling that purchasing your service or product is perfectly consistent with what has already been done. You should take the initiative to point this out *before* the contrary claim is uttered by the buyer.

Professional Benefit

The typical telemarketer appeals to a prospect's presumed need to make his or her professional life more efficient. The assumption here is that the buyer is a rational animal who will evaluate offers and determine if the proposed deal is really *beneficial* to his or her company or household.

In this spirit, salespeople have been taught over the last several years to sell "benefits" and not just sell "features." A benefit is what something will do for someone, while a feature is some aspect of the product or service.

For instance, an ice-cream cone may have a scoop of chocolate on it. This is a feature of the product, or one of the attributes the product possesses. If I say that the chocolate ice-cream will satisfy your sweet tooth, I am now telling you what the product will do for you, and this is an important benefit. It is claimed that people really "buy benefits," and are only secondarily interested in features.

In order to avoid selling the wrong benefits, it is wise to determine in advance which benefits are likely to be most appealing to the prospect and then to refer to those benefits during the conversation.

Personal Needs and Values

People derive personal satisfactions from the purchases they make, even if they occur at the workplace. For instance, a receptionist who orders a telephone headset which improves her efficiency not only benefits on a professional level, but may also come to regard her purchase as enhancing her sense of self, or self-esteem.

She can have several personal satisfactions, and here is a list of some of the payoffs she can garner for herself through this action:

1. *She can see herself as a professional person.* In deciding to buy the device she has executed an independent action which demonstrates that she is aware of the need for self-improvement. This is one mark of a pro. She will feel a continuing need to grow and will seek avenues appropriate to expressing and satisfying this need.

2. *She can compliment herself for doing something "smart."* All of us wish to see ourselves as intelligent. A seemingly small investment, such as buying a headset, can be viewed as a really bright move if it results in heightened job performance.

3. *She can feel more secure in her job.* Save a company money and they'll usually show loyalty toward you, thus increasing your job security.

4. *She can feel heightened family security.* As her job becomes more secure, her family may become more financially and emotionally secure as well.

These are just some of the personal needs and values that can be reinforced by purchasing a product that enhances productivity. *While there may be dozens of individual motives that can be aroused, such as those mentioned above, your goal is to associate your product or service with at least one such motive in order to anchor the prospect's personality to the buying decision.*

For a thorough discussion of the twenty-one values that you can appeal to when speaking with a customer, see pages 81-89 in *Selling Skills for the Nonsalesperson* (Prentice-Hall, 1984).

Putting It all Together

Now that we've discussed the various ways that we can appeal to the customer's motives, let's put together a few examples to illustrate the process.

Appeal #1:
Instilling Fear

Let's say that you're going to sell this book, *Gary Goodman's 60-Second Salesperson*, to prospects and you want to appeal to a person's need to avoid fearful outcomes. Assume, for the purpose of the example, that you have already moved through the first twenty seconds of the call, and have therefore announced yourself and your company.

You are now beginning your description of this wonderful book, and what you want to point out is how useful it is to have a guide for *quickly* presenting sales messages to prospects.

> "Perhaps the most important benefit of the book is the way it shows salespeople how to avoid wasting valuable time with people who have no intention of buying in the first place."

> "We all know that time is money, and when we're stuck in the middle of a long presentation with no way out, we can see our paychecks shrinking with each passing minute ..."

Note how this fear appeal is rather mild, yet poignant. I don't tell the customer that he or she is losing money right now, but instead I leave it to her to tell herself that she is as I make my appeal.

Furthermore, I link my fear message to a truism that no one would deny: Time is money. You'll find that when you start with a readily accepted belief and proceed to "prove" your following thought through the introduction of this belief, you will arouse much more swift acceptance of your ideas than you might otherwise. People find themselves agreeing with something that sounds totally acceptable and tend to gloss over the next claim they hear.

Notice the words that are used in the second portion of the fear appeal. The prospect is told he or she is "stuck" with "no way out," while helplessly watching the awful spectacle of a "shrinking" paycheck. If you look at these terms by themselves, you feel like the victims in some terrifying sci-fi movie.

Again, recall that you are dissecting a process here which can make you think that your strategy will be visible to the buyer. In practice, it shouldn't work this way at all. A properly written fear message will really do its work without bringing undue attention to the message or the speaker's techniques.

I sense that fear appeals can work best with generally insecure people, many of whom are used to making decisions on the basis of *avoidance of negativity*. If you find that you are dealing with someone who generally avoids decisions, or who seems to view events and proposals pessimistically, your best approach may be through the fear message. Here is why: They may never "get off the dime" if you appeal to the prospect of positive gain, because they can't really relate to it on a personal level. If all such people can see is the prospect of potential loss when their most cherished wish is to preserve the *status quo*, they'll be excellent candidates for minor fear appeals.

Appeal #2: "It's Just Like You to Buy a Book Like This!"

When you appeal to someone's need for cognitive consistency you are really holding up a mirror of the person's or company's past in order to justify the present buying decision.

> "*Gary Goodman's 60-Second Salesperson* will fit in beautifully with your philosophy of time management and maximizing resource utilization.
>
> "In fact, this book will do for telemarketing what you people have so successfully done in other areas ..."

If it feels like you are selling "to ego" here, it's true. There has been much written during the last few years about "corporate culture," and the ways in which companies represent certain operating philosophies which are very successfully diffused to all levels of employees and throughout all regions in which the firms operate. By observing and discussing a company's past actions and attitudes, especially if they represent cornerstones of the corporate culture, you can ingratiate yourself while linking your wares to the collective ego with which you are dealing.

Appeal #3: Professional Enhancement

When you appeal to professional enhancement, you are summoning benefits that usually relate to a company's ability to make or save money through your services. Consequently, these appeals tend to be rather straightforward.

> "*Gary Goodman's 60-Second Salesperson* will show your salespeople how to close orders in less time than they ever thought possible while helping them to contact at least three times the number of

people they normally speak to. All of this adds up to greater efficiency and a greater return on your investment ..."

It helps an appeal when you can somehow *quantify* the results that will accrue to the listener. These become "mental hooks," upon which the customer places a lot of confidence.

Notice that I repeat the word, "greater" in the second portion of this segment. This is done for a reason: I want to build a feeling of momentum in the sales talk at this point, because I will be moving toward structuring my offer in the next ten seconds of the presentation.

Appeal #4:
Offering a Personal Reward

Sometimes you will find it necessary to appeal to people's individual motivations to make a deal. Often, this is in situations where the buyer doesn't stand to benefit financially from a particular transaction, and therefore doesn't have very much ego-involvement in who gets the business.

In cases such as these, you need to break through the apathy in the situation and try to find a salient motive that you can arouse in the buyer.

Let's say that a secretary has been asked to speak with you about buying this book. What could a secretary know about telemarketing? Probably very little, and this is all the more reason that you should actively pursue the development of an appeal that will cause this person to become involved with the project.

Here's how I might structure the talk at this point:

"One of the major benefits of *Gary Goodman's 60-Second Salesperson* is that it shows how to cut down on wasted calls and wasted paperwork that goes along with them. This means that you will probably be a lot freer from having to process a lot of wasteful letters and follow up contacts ..."

Again, I am repeating key words. "Waste" is one of them. I am assuming that secretaries are profoundly biased against waste and sloppiness, and if they have a chance to stamp out these evils, even if they are in someone else's department, they'll go right ahead and do it on principle.

I am also hoping that the secretary will have to "touch" the paper flow from selling efforts at various points, and if I can make his or her job easier it will help me to make a sale.

The third ten seconds is critical to your success because it is here that you get into the nitty-gritty of your call. In presenting your product or service at this time you are creating the essence of the sales talk by raising advantages to which the prospect must relate if you are to be successful.

You are now about to formulate your offer, which will "open your hand" entirely to the prospect, revealing both what you want and what obligations this will create for the listener. It is to this exciting and vulnerable fourth ten seconds that we will turn next.

The third 10 seconds in review:

1. Remember: products don't sell themselves; people who make them attractive do.
2. Salespeople commit five classic errors in describing products and services:
   * They take too much time.
   * They get overly technical.
   * They assume too much knowledge or interest.
   * They may sound overly laudatory.
   * They may damn their products with faint praise.
3. What you think you are selling may not be what customers think they are buying. What you think is beneficial may not be perceived as beneficial by the customer.
4. Buying decisions are usually based upon four motives:
   * Fear.
   * Cognitive consistency.
   * Professional benefits.
   * Personal needs and values.

5

The Fourth 10 Seconds
Fashioning the Offer

A telephone "offer" is perhaps the most delicate portion of the entire sales process. This is the point in the call when you get down to the nitty-gritty, where the customer sharpens his or her pencil as well as buying instincts, and where you will receive much of your resistance. It is here, during the fourth ten seconds, that you will either win the poker hand or simply "go busted."

Unfortunately, the products and services that are sold by phone do not have neat little price tags to which a curious or interested buyer may turn to determine the offering price. As we know, pricetags tend to seem very definite to the prospect, who recognizes that the same price is being charged to all customers because the fee is visible.

When selling by phone, you don't have the standard retailing tricks of the trade, such as price tags, that can denote a standard pricing scheme and, by implication, set forth an aura of honesty around the seller. Accordingly, you don't have banners proclaiming "Half-Price Sale" and "Extraordinary Value" and "Clearance," as you encounter in aggressive stores.

You only have those tools that have assisted us during the preceding thirty seconds of the conversation: your words and your voice. This isn't to say that your equipment is necessarily deficient, because it isn't. If you are resourceful, you can fashion offers that are both "hard to refuse" and that make good sense for all parties involved in the transaction.

Putting Customers into the Mood to Buy

Have you ever noticed how you behave immediately after you get some really good news? When I get great news I'm usually floating on air for a period of time, and I've come to realize that both my outlook and my communication style change during that time.

I become much more enthusiastic about everything. Mundane tasks take on a delightful cast, and for the shortest time I can do "no wrong."

During these periods of grace, I often call my toughest prospects and customers because I know that nothing they say or do will bring me down from my "high." In fact, during these spontaneous bursts I often end up making tremendous strides that I wouldn't have otherwise if it weren't for my altered view and approach to things.

Customers operate exactly as you do. They like to make buying decisions within a certain atmosphere. At the same time, if the buying climate is too forbidding, they will wait for a more appropriate environment in which to plunk down their dollars.

I'm this way in department stores. If I am comfortable with the place and the salespeople I am capable of buying myself a year's wardrobe on one outing. By the same logic, if I am put off by something, I'll pass up some of the sales of the century.

What behaviors on the part of the seller are responsible for putting customers into a buying mood? Here are several tips for what to say and do:

Be Assumptive

Customers expect to be led into buying decisions by expert guides. What you need to do is exert leadership and let customers know exactly what is expected of them.

Here's what I mean: Left to their own devices, prospects will not make affirmative buying decisions with nearly the same frequency that they will when they are "talked into it" by a seller. By being talked into it I am not advocating the "spray and pray" approach to selling, whereby you nearly talk the customer to death while spewing forth buying advantages which may hit or miss the mark.

You need to take on a tone of voice that tells the customer that you are sure he or she will want to buy. Why would you be speaking to each other if a sale weren't likely to result from your efforts?

Salespeople are neither educators nor public servants; they are persuaders. They are responsible for moving products and services that wouldn't move off the shelves were it not for their efforts.

This is to say that salespeople need to develop scripts as well as phone manners that convey tremendous confidence to the potential buyer. This means that we have to sell ourselves before making every call in order to be able to command the allegiance of the customer to our cause.

Be Simple

The phone doesn't seem geared for offers that get overly technical. Because customers cannot see the deal in black and white, you can't rely on them to make sense of a lot of verbal fine print that is flying past them at a rate of 200 words per minute.

There are two tips that have been handed down to salespeople through the ages that are appropriate here: "Make your product attractive to the customer, and make it easy to buy."

The ease-of-buying quality cannot be underestimated. I recall selling credit cards several years ago to potential customers of department stores. What we did was get on the phones every day of the week, including Sunday afternoon, and announce that the listener had been selected to receive a much-coveted charge card from a prominent store. People were thrilled to feel that their credit was good enough to warrant our attention, and some eighty percent accepted the charge privilege we offered.

There was practically no reason to refuse our offer because the customers had to take very little action to enjoy the benefits we extended. All they had to do was help us to update our credit profile by giving us recent information about their place of employment, home ownership status, and the like.

While I recognize that our sale in this case was less ambitious than many selling tasks that you may take on, the fundamental maxim of keeping the offer simple applies to whatever you are selling.

Along this line, I suggest you keep your language very simple and free of ambiguity. Short words with direct meanings will tell the buyer that you are completely upfront in your dealings and that there is no reason to search for concealed information or to hesitate to buy from you.

Remember this simple truth: The longer you talk about anything, the more complex the offer will seem to the buyer. Be a person of few words as you approach the fourth ten seconds.

Be Subtle

As I have noted in my other books, the offer brings with it a great deal of tension for both buyer and seller when the transaction is conducted traditionally. This tension is also a manifestation of *defensiveness*, which occurs when the parties to a conversation feel that they are coming under attack; each party makes an effort to shield him- or herself from threat while possibly launching a counterattack aimed at his or her adversary.

This is nasty business, and this is probably the least satisfying part of the selling game for all concerned. There are ways to defuse the explosiveness that can accompany this period in the transaction. To appreciate these corrective measures we should first look into what ordinarily takes place that arouses defensiveness.

On the Seller's Side

Salespeople grow very nervous as they approach the stage when they are about to make the offer. This is understandable because they expect to hear a lot of objections and avoidance maneuvers on the part of prospects. All too often, seller's *project* their own uncertainty and even hostility onto an otherwise neutral prospect. Then, after sensing negativity from the salesperson, the prospect *reflects* the bad attitude that's being conveyed. This begins a cycle of defense and attack which ordinarily culminates in a lost sale, and perhaps embitters the parties to the transaction.

It *is* understandable that the typical seller would be nearly cringing as he or she makes the offer known because the person has probably heard so much rejection in the past at this critical stage in the talk that he or she has become conditioned to expect a negative reception from the buyer.

What you need to do, of course, is decondition yourself and set into place a new mental program that assures you that there is a high probability of the person saying "yes" instead of "no."

I can't tell you how many times I have trained new telemarketers, seen them get their first order, often without any customer resistance, and then heard these suddenly successful people exclaim, "I could have sworn he was going to say 'no.'" It's lucky that our projections don't always come true!

Sellers, having had so many past rejections, can easily become *angry* with prospects with whom thay have never spoken. Here's how it works:

Imagine that you have been battered about by one negative prospect after another, and that you are about to reach out and "touch" yet another one. At this point, it's more likely that you want to reach out and *crunch* them. In this situation, most of us cannot help but convey our irritation with past customers to prospective ones.

I call this process "call contamination," and like a very nasty infection, it can prey upon the innocent and prevent you from being as effective as you should be. A good way to combat this malady is to take at least one deep breath between your phone calls to create a sense of mental separation between your contacts. This will remind you that each call constitutes a whole new experience and that you should allow each one to stand on its own, unaffected by any others that may have preceded it.

How Sellers Cause Defensiveness

Sellers cause defensiveness in a number of ways as they move into the offer. One way is by sounding highly *strategic* with the customer. If you sound as if you are attempting to conceal something, or if you are being vague in your articulation of the deal, customers will naturally recoil and create distance between themselves and the seller. Frankly, none of us wishes to be manipulated, and if we sense that something of the sort is going on, we'll defeat the sales effort.

Sellers can also come on too strongly with the prospect, making the listener feel that the deal is too good to be true. What's happening here is a situation in which the seller seems *too certain*, or overly confident in his claims.

One of my clients says that he has a refined "b.s. detector" that goes off like a fire alarm whenever he hears unduly optimistic claims from salespeople. I learned of this fascinating device when I was speaking to him one day about some accomplishment and he apparently grew weary of hearing my self-congratulatory references.

"Beep ... beep ... beep ... beep," he suddenly broadcast, in the middle of one of my phrases. After I asked him why he was making these strange noises, he informed me of the existence of his magical protective alarm system.

Sellers can cause defensiveness in customers by sounding as if they "are only out for themselves." It is very important to convey the feeling that you have a genuine interest in the well-being of the prospect. If you fail to sound customer-oriented, this will be interpreted as *neutrality*, or "I-couldn't-care-less-about-you" attitude. Who would want to buy in this situation?

Defensiveness can also be aroused if you give the impression that you dislike the customer. Most of us like to feel that we are somewhat hard-boiled, and that it takes quite a bit of direct negativity to distract us from a businesslike purpose, such as purchasing something.

Not true. Any subtle suggestion on the part of the seller that he or she doesn't like us can make us feel that he or she is being *negatively evaluated*, and who wants to feel that he or she is being criticized when he or she is about to invest in a particular purchase?

A negative evaluation of this sort may be conveyed through a sound of impatience. If the customer asks a reasonable question, and the seller responds as if to say, "That was a really dumb interruption," who wouldn't be put off by this kind of treatment?

Of course, there is another side of the coin: the customer's. Customers aren't "babes in the woods" when it comes to making purchases. By adulthood, most of us have made thousands of small and large purchases, and often these have been made after interacting with a salesperson.

So we know what someone is up to when he or she describes a product or service to us over the phone. It's clear that the person is after a sale, and we have been taught since childhood that "being taken to the cleaners" by some silver-tongued seller is something to be avoided at all costs.

One of the games customers play when you are moving into your offer is something I call the "Ralph Nader Game." Most prospects, in order to earn their merit badges as good consumers, feel obligated to offer up at least one penetrating question or pointed objection before relenting to a wily seller.

Often, these utterances seem less than completely genuine. A well-heeled person will claim that he "can't afford it," and you may know better. This may cause you to grow defensive because you'll see the ruse as being *strategic*, which was noted before as a cause of tension between buyer and seller.

A customer may say, "I don't have time." This could be true or it could be just another excuse to get you off the line. In fact, you may know that your talk will be finished in a matter of seconds and realize that the prospect is clearly wrong in his claim about having to rush off the phone. This can mke you feel that you are being *negatively evaluated* and being called, by implication, "a time waster."

What about people who don't even hear the offer but still claim that they won't be interested? How can they know at this point? Did they consult a crystal ball? Read tea leaves? Look to their morning horoscopes? This type can irk you because they seem so *certain* without having heard any evidence to support their contentions.

What Can We Do About It?

Obviously, defensiveness cuts both ways. As they say, the winner in any particular fight is the one who sits the contest out.

This means that you should avoid sending defensive messages to the extent possible, and when you hear a customer's defensive ploys, you should calm yourself and instruct yourself to stay in control of the situation by not overreacting. Just because a comment has made you defensive in the past does not mean that it must produce the same result in you in the present and future.

For a thorough discussion of defensiveness and conflict-reduction techniques, see *Winning by Telephone,* (Prentice-Hall, 1982); for a complete analysis of how to address objections and manage resistance, see *You Can Sell Anything by Telephone! (Prentice-Hall, 1984).*

What Should You Sound Like as You Move into the Offer?

You now know that your voice should not sound defensive or as if you are in any way attacking the customer. But, what should you sound like as you move into the fourth ten seconds of your sales talk?

You should sound *friendly, spontaneous,* and *simple.* Let's look at these attributes in a little detail.

When we're friendly with someone our voices sound rather light and breezy, instead of heavy and highly guarded. We also seem to convey a "telephone smile" as we are talking that sends a "relationship message" to the prospect, saying, "I like speaking with you." In addition, we tend to inject our conversation with spicier feedback in response to the other party's comments. By spicer, I don't mean that you simply say "uh-huh" in a very bored way with each passing sentence. Instead, you should issue what psychologists call "therapeutic grunts," that send an additional message of positive regard to the speaker. "I see," and "really," and "what do you know," are some of the many phrases that encourage the speaker to open up to you and build a positive telephone relationship.

Spontaneity is very important in building bridges with potential customers. When you seem spontaneous, you are causing the prospect to trust you. You are doing the opposite of sounding strategic, which, as you have seen, is a factor in arousing defensivesness.

You don't have to come across as if you are "off the wall" to be received as being spontaneous. By simply allowing your natural enthusiasm to percolate through the converstion you'll find that your exchanges take on a much livelier nature, and prospects tend to find your offers very reasonable and quite normal.

As mentioned earlier in this chapter, it pays to sound simple when you are at the offer stage of your talk. Sometimes, your delivery can help you make an otherwise slightly complex offer easier to understand. By slowing down when you are mentioning the dollars involved in the transaction, you will arouse customer confidence by sending a signal that *you* are secure with the financial side of the deal.

Speaking of the financial side of matters, how should you build your text at this critical stage in the presentation? We'll turn to this topic next as we explore the development of the offer, per se.

How Would Dean Martin Do It?

There are a few people who have established themselves as superstars with certain polished images, and one such luminary is Dean Martin.

There's no question that this guy is *smooth*. Listen to one of his records or watch him in a movie and you will be listening to or looking at someone who could have invented the word charisma.

I recall seeing him at a Little League game where his son was pitching, and the fellow looked great: yellow pants, a pink shirt, and pink suede shoes with yellow socks. Dean Martin is the only guy in the world who could have worn that crazy color combination and produced honest admiration in everyone who saw him.

On another occasion I was riding along with a friend in Beverly Hills when we spotted Dino driving a Mercedes. I was embarrassed as my friend shouted out at the celebrity who calmly raised his hand in front of the rear view mirror and waved it like he owned the planet. What a cool person! He accepted a crude shout as if it were a golden tribute.

Now, why does Dean Martin come to mind when I think of putting together the offer? His image envelops me because the offer should have the same sense of fluid momentum that this personality exhibits. You shouldn't put together the offer as if it is an alien treatise that is sure to turn the listener off, but rather as an integrated part of the whole presentation that comes across clearly, yet unobtrusively.

Here is one of the best ways of setting forth an offer:

"What we're doing is ..."

In these four words you have started to change the world. What you've done here is set your offer into motion through your choice of words. "What we're doing" denotes a process of change that is well under way. It also says that "we" are the actors in the drama, and at this particular point in the talk the customer doesn't know if this includes him or her or if it only involves the company of the speaker. Nonetheless, it reinforces the feeling that something is going on with a quality of inevitability about it that one individual wouldn't want to impede.

By making your offer sound alive and kinetic you are sweeping up the customer in a wave of change that seems mildly dramatic, yet pleasing. This language allows the customer to be passive in the transaction and to simply prepare to offer assent when you arrive at the close.

Note that I have not chosen to say, "What we'd like to do is this," because this would force the customer to approve our conduct before I have mentioned what it is going to be. By using "like to," you would be asking permission to engage in an action that you should simply proceed to embark upon without first checking for assent. For a complete discussion of language to avoid using, see *Reach Out & Sell Someone*, (Prentice-Hall, 1983).

Selling "On Approval"

It is difficult to induce customers to "sign on the dotted line" when speaking on the phone because they often can't see any agreement before them. This makes it impractical to close the deal in a traditional way.

One good way to get around this problem is to consider sealing the deal by sending the product to the customer on a trial or approval basis. You'll find that a number of people will really be "lookylous," who won't have a serious interest in retaining your product on a paid basis, and many of these people will return it after they have toyed with it.

Some of your competitors will allow you to send them your wares so they can analyze your shipping methods, enclosures, follow-up methods, and dissect your product, all at your expense. When you realize the nefarious purposes to which your approval selling is put, you may determine that you don't want to withstand the frustration that comes from having to process returned orders while wading through numerous bogus excuses for reversing deals.

I recognize that I may not be painting a very pretty picture of approval selling, but it does have its merits. With the insecure buyer, this method may be just the trick that is needed to convince the person that your product has merit and should be tried. In a way, I suppose, the approval method is similar to being given a taste of a new product while shopping in a supermarket in the hope that you'll like it and buy some on the spot. If people don't have an opportunity to *safely* explore the merit of your wares, how can they be expected to go along with an appeal to buy?

This points out the need for some kind of escape hatch for the customer who is trying out a new product and who would otherwise not consider buying it on her own. I understand that during its early years in the United States, Subaru couldn't give away its automobile franchises. Apparently, this auto company nearly had to beg existing American dealers to place one or two of its cars in their showrooms. As you know, Subaru has become yet another success story among import car manufacturers.

In many situations the existence of a return privilege will provide enough additional sales to justify the problems associated with managing a certain percentage of returns. When I was in the book business about fifteen years ago, we found that approximately 50 percent of those who were sent general interest books after being sold by phone ultimately returned them. We knew, however, what the margins were going to be, and we figured that the buyers would go on to purchase an average of three books apiece, which would more than make up for our returns.

The approval format is especially useful when you have to move out a lot of product in a short period of time. This sales approach guarantees a certain amount of enthusiasm on the salesperson's part, and allows you to make the claim that you stand behind your product.

Approval selling isn't limited to small items, either. Kroy sells a line of machines that help firms to do the sort of layout work in formulating brochures and printed matter that would otherwise be done by expensive typesetters. What this firm does is contact prospects and ship each one a machine. The prospects set up the machines on their desks, and the Kroy telemarketer calls them and "walks them through" the procedures involved in using the device. Kroy has found this demonstration formula to be quite effective, yet it is surprising that more firms haven't exploited the potential of this sort of marketing.

Language Considerations

When building the offer there are a few rules pertaining to language that should be followed:

1. Minimize the expense through "buffer terms."
2. Always follow a negative statement with a positive one.
3. Mention the price well before you ask for the sale.

You need to use some of the same phraseology that has come to be expected when we read space advertising: *"Reduced to* only $1995" would be the sort of phrase that might play very well during a phone presentation. People love bargains, and when something has been "reduced," many feel that there is a certain amount of urgency in the situation which can be turned to their advantage by making a quick, yet prudent purchase.

Similarly, "only $1995" tells the prospect how to regard the price of $1995. If you simply uttered the price in all of its starkness, it is probable that the customer would not have a frame of reference through which he or she could evaluate the reasonableness of the offer. Your inclusion of "only" is a clear signal that says this price is reasonable and represents a good value.

When you have mentioned the price, you may not wish to leave the customer thinking it over, because price alone seldom sells anything. Accordingly, you should realize that mentioning the cost is usually not a "plus" in anyone's mind, yet you have to mention it to be able to create an acceptance of your offer. So, what you should do is state the price and then follow it with a statement of advantage or benefit to the customer.

For instance, you may say:

> "This marvelous widget is only $1995, which represents a tremendous value in terms of the years of service it will give you."

What this technique does is take the sting out of the cost of the item by immediately shifting the attention of the buyer to a significant advantage that will be derived.

Never do you want to "close" on price. For instance, I would not say:

> "And this marvelous widget is only $1995, *Okay?*"

What this does is place undue emphasis upon the cost and the listener is probably going to be unnecessarily preoccupied with this dimension of the offer, even if the price is reasonable.

In the next chapter we'll look at various ways that you can engineer consent in the fifth ten seconds of your presentation.

The fourth 10 seconds in review:

1. To make an offer attractive, you should put the customer into the right buying mood by:
   - Being assumptive.
   - Making a simple offer that is easy to follow.
   - Overcoming customer and seller defensiveness.
2. When making the offer, you need to sound *friendly, spontaneous,* and *simple.*
3. To ease the customer's concern about the offering stage in the presentation, you should strive to sound *smooth* and make the offer flow easily from the preceding portion of the talk.
4. *Selling on approval* is an effective means of introducing a new

product, generating a lot of sales during a short period, and dramatizing the product's benefits through actual customer demonstrations.

The drawback to selling on approval is the rather high percentage of returns that must be processed.

5. The offer requires that your *language* be such that it:

- Minimizes the perception of the expensive nature of your products.
- Requires you to follow a negative statement with a positive one, as when you mention the price of an item.
- Requires you to mention the price of your product *well before you close.*

6

The Fifth 10 Seconds
Creating Commitment

When somebody asks us to do something for them, what kinds of mental changes do most of us go through? It seems to me that I:

1. Feel threatened right away because the request may be something that I had not thought I would be accosted with at that particular moment.
2. Ask myself if there is anything standing in the way of my performing the requested act.
3. Ask myself if I really want to do it.
4. Ask myself if I *owe it* to the requester to honor the appeal.
5. Try to determine if my response will place me in jeopardy.
6. Attune my response to fit the relationship I have had and hope to have with the person who asked me to act in the first place.

You may agree that I go through a lot of machinations before responding verbally and I think I am like most people in this regard. When you attempt to secure commitment to a proposal you are entering a complex mental environment, and you had better be prepared to negotiate it properly.

You may find that the fifth ten seconds of the telemarketing process is the most butterfly-producing, hair-raising, and uncomfortable part of the telemarketing venture. It doesn't have to be, though. It can even be fun if you are in charge of yourself and have a toolbox of effective closing techniques.

Closing Is a
Winning Habit

When should you set forth to close a prospect? According to the pros, you should be closing from word one.

Here's what I mean: Closing requires that the seller express the same sort of assumptive attitude that was noted in the last chapter. He or she needs to begin the talk with a tone of "inevitablity" that says, "You're going to buy from me, sooner or later."

The call must also convey the feeling that the seller isn't just playing around as he or she moves through the presentation. And most importantly, the seller must shape the message as if it is a series of mini-closes.

This accustoms the prospect to hearing closing questions and responding appropriately. For instance, if I want to enlist the support of a buyer for my overall idea I may do this by producing a small agreement to begin with. For example:

> "And you know, Mr. Johnson, our products have been directly responsible for increasing sales effectiveness by over 100 percent; that's pretty good, isn't it?"

By endorsing your success and its desirability, the prospect is beginning to nod in agreement as you progress through the call. The habit of agreeing with minor aspects of the talk leads the prospect into agreeing with the proposal in its entirety.

This technique, like any other, can backfire if you use too many closes in rapid succession that bring undue attention to themselves. Accordingly, you should be careful to use these mini-closes at strategic points in the call where they seem to be spoken spontaneously, thus catching the listener by surprise.

Learn by Doing

How do you come to be a great closer? Through practice and more practice, until closing becomes such a part of you that you find yourself closing for commitment in all sorts of strange situations, such as restaurants, when you want a nice table or certain specially prepared foods.

I am also a believer in the idea that closing becomes a nearly unconscious activity when you have had extensive selling background.

One of my clients was speaking to someone in his office recently when he used one of the best closing lines I had ever heard. After listening to his counterpart hold forth about the difficulties involved in pursuing a project, my friend asked:

"What's the alternative?"

Isn't that a beautiful question? It nearly blew me off my seat when I heard it!

In my view, it has a number of strengths:

1. It's short and snappy.
2. It's nondefensive.
3. It focuses the listener's attention upon only one critical issue preliminary to coming to agreement.

I also appreciate the assumption contained in this simple question: That is, "We're going to move ahead on this project, and we have one acceptable plan before us, and if you can't supply a valid alternative, then we're going to have to move ahead with it as it is .. ."

Three Closes That Work Beautifully Over the Phone

I have worked with three closes over the years that have proven very effective over the phone: The assumptive close, the checkback close, and the choice close. I'll go over these in detail for you.

The assumptive close doesn't really *ask* for anything from the listener: it tells them what is going to happen. For instance, I may engineer an assumptive close with the following words:

> "What we're doing is stopping by to obtain the written approvals and the best time to arrange this will be Tuesday, the 25th, between three and four. That'll also give us an opportunity to say hello and bring ourselves up to date on the account."

Note what I *didn't* do here. I didn't ask if it would be acceptable to obtain signatures, or even if the time I elected was convenient. I simply stated what *will* work out well for all concerned.

I am assuming commitment with this approach, and it will take an overt, assertive response on the part of the prospect to stop the ball that has been rolling to the point where he or she will have a chance to enter the conversation.

You may be thinking that this sort of close is too forceful, and it may be in certain situations. For instance, with very dogmatic people you may elect to soft-pedal matters a bit and refrain from excessive assumptiveness, which could be interpreted as a direct challenge to an authoritarian personality.

At the same time, be aware of the power of this close, particularly when handling prospects possessing average sensibilities. One tip to keep in mind is to make your voice sound nonstressed and light, and this will compensate for wording which may seem a little brusque.

The checkback close takes much of the sting out of the assumptive close by adding a crucial "escape hatch" for the prospect by checking for his approval. Here's how you modify the assumptive approach to turn it into a checkback close:

> "What we're doing is stopping by to obtain the written approvals and the best time to arrange this will be Tuesday, the 25th, between three and four. That'll also give us an opportunity to say hello and bring ourselves up to date on the account, *okay?*"

What did you detect that was different in this revised version? If you said I added the word "okay" at the end, you're right. This word is one of the best little moneymakers you'll ever find. It produces commitment quickly while cutting through the maze of indecision that afflicts most buyers.

"Okay?," is a question that most of us are taught by experience to respond to automatically, without giving deep consideration to the import of the answer we are giving. Because "okay" is used so much by speakers who are simply trying to elicit feedback from us as we speak, we are also predisposed positively toward giving them what they are asking for, and that is acknowledgement. In this situation, of course, we are also giving them consent to the proposal that has been outlined in the call.

There are several phrases that can be used to make your "checkbacks" come across in a very casual way. For instance, you can ask; "Sounds good, doesn't it?" I love this phrase because it encourages the person to agree with your judgment before you have even gotten to the "doesn't it" part.

Another good phrase is, "That'll work out well, won't it?" Note that *you* are providing the overall perspective through which the customer is asked to view whatever it is that you are referring to at the moment, whether it is the last point you made in the talk or the entire proposal. When you frame things in this way, what else can the listener do but agree with you? It's really a very simple way of engineering consent, isn't it?

I just did it to you with the last sentence of the last paragraph, didn't I? Oh my gosh, there it goes again, right? Oh no, this could become habit forming, couldn't it? Help! I can't stop, can I?

You get the point. You can string these along and actually condition the prospect to "finish" your ideas for you before you have verbalized your conclusions, *can't you?* You're really going to use the checkback close, _____ _____?

The third type of close that I have found very effective over the phone is the choice close, which admittedly has been around for years, yet it has also been misused in many cases. The choice close attempts to have the customer feel that he or she is making a choice in the transaction, yet his or her decision is: (1) Limited to two alternatives; (2) Narrowed to electing one item or the other, and not "neither;" and (3) Often restricted to a minor point.

By modifying the example that I have used to illustrate the last two closes, I'll show you how the choice close works:

> "What we're doing is stopping by to obtain the written approvals and the best time to arrange this will be Tuesday, the 25th, between three and four, or will the 26th work out better for you?"

I haven't asked the person *whether* he or she wishes me to stop by, but *when*. This makes the listener feel that stopping by to obtain approvals is totally natural and constitutes the proper "next step" in the transaction.

By limiting the prospect's choices, you're shaping the desired response while disallowing too much time for wasteful reflection. By offering two choices, you're also removing from consideration the probability that the person will elect neither alternative, or not to buy, altogether.

The choice close enables you to secure commitment on a minor point as well. You know that I don't really care very much if I receive the contracts on one day or the next, in many cases, but providing the illusion of choice to the buyer is a wise way of allowing the person to feel some sense of control, yet not so much as to feel sufficiently emboldened to walk away from the deal.

Unobtrusive Closing

There are certain prospects who are very ego-involved in the decision process, and some salespeople have called these kinds of prospects "drivers." They express a very strong need to drive the call to a conclusion, and if you get in their way, they'll retard your progress toward a close.

When encountering these people, and others who may feel that they "aren't your typical buyer," but are head and shoulders above most prospects, one of the best things to do is to induce them to close themselves.

I know you've heard the expression that says that if you "give 'em enough rope," they'll do themselves in. This certainly can apply to giving over a certain degree of control to prospects so they'll persuade themselves to buy.

This doesn't mean that you should create a mental state known as "disinformation." When someone is placed into a mental atmosphere of disinformation, he or she becomes confused and distrustful of his or her senses. What this means in the selling context is that the prospect can feel that there is no structure to the sales process, grow restless, and terminate the conversation.

Disinformation can come from turning over too much control to the buyer. For instance, if I called a prospect and announced the name of my company and immediately told the person that I thought we should be doing business, this would miscue the listener, who would probably think of a dozen good reasons why we should do no such thing.

There *is* something to be said for creating a moderate amount of uncertainty, though. One theory of psychology holds that people strive for *homeostasis*, or mental balance, in most things that they do. They try to be consistent, or at least to appear to themselves and others in this way.

When a seller causes a prospect to feel uncertain, the latter usually does what he or she can to restore balance to the situation; often he or she will create structure where there was none, and do it in a way which really helps the seller.

The 20-Second Presentation, with Close

Throughout this book you've probably been wondering whether I could really build a sales talk that lasted only sixty seconds. Well, would you believe that I have done a lot better that that? That's right, I've developed a sales talk that lasts only twenty seconds or so. The novelty of this approach is its use of the uncertainty principle outlined above.

To spread my seminars across the country, I determined that the best way to dramatize my method was to use it on highly resistant prospects. I chose some of the toughest "birds" around, including stodgy college deans and stuffy executives. I set forth to contact as many of these people as I could within a short period and invite them to cosponsor my seminars. Here's how my call went:

> "Hello, Mr. Wilson? This is Dr. Gary Goodman calling; I've developed some very successful seminars in the area of telephone marketing, and the reason I'm calling is to determine how to pursue the prospect of bringing them to your organization ..."

Simple, right? Absolutely. And this presentation is very much built on a soft-selling concept. The key to the pitch is found in the last phrase which tells the person that I am calling "to determine how to pursue the prospect of bringing them to your organization."

Please note that I used a particularly soft phrase in the words, "pursue the prospect." I didn't ask, "How can we do some business?," nor did I ask, "How can we stage these programs at the corporation you have there?"

"Pursue the prospect" implies that the call is exploratory, and I don't expect to wrap this thing up over the phone. This creates a very helpful illusion because I certainly expect to close on the first call. The trick lies in setting the listener's fears to rest while creating the kind of rich informational exchange that will result in a commitment. Well, what happens after I have done my twenty-second "special?" The listener usually feels obliged to set before me a sales path which helps us to plan the remainder of the persuasive method.

For example, I'll often hear something to the effect of: "Well, it would be helpful to see something in writing ..." This is a very important moment in the exchange because you could interpret the request for literature as an excuse, stall, or objection, which it could be in many other sorts of presentations, but it isn't here.

All you need to do is respond by promising, "I'll be happy to, and what you'll see will be some testimonials as well as publicity that will show you ..." This sets the person at ease, and literally disarms him or her as you continue the persuasive procedure.

You may continue by asking, "Assuming all is in order, what is the next step?" This gets you down to the nitty-gritty as it advances the relationship by reducing the mystery involved in bringing the project to life. If the client is going to support your efforts, he or she will try to map the remaining territory that needs to be traversed before you have reached your selling target. If the client is resistant or less than genuinely supportive, he or she may hedge and try to plead ignorance and fall back to waiting to see the materials before committing him- or herself to further involvement.

In the great majority of circumstances, however, you'll find prospects helping you out by saying that they believe the next step should be either closing the deal or doing some kind of act that is the equivalent of closing the deal.

When selling my seminars, I noticed that setting dates for

the programs was the key buying signal that I was headed toward, and when the prospect mentioned that this was the next step I would simply agree and suggest we do it right away to assure that the dates would be available when required.

When we had established the dates the conversation normally turned to promotion and compensation, which are subjects near and dear to me, of course. By the time these topics had been handled, I knew that the sale was, for all intents and purposes, closed.

The mailed materials would restate the agreement we had made by covering the dates of the programs, the dollars involved, promotional media to be employed, and so forth. All the prospect then had to do was sign the bottom line and return the letter to me. Easy, right?

I should point out that my twenty-second presentation actually lasts for several minutes, once the listeners start selling themselves. For the most part, however, the initial persuasion really takes place during my brief overture to the prospects when I enlist their help in telling me how to sell them.

The "Where Did I Go Wrong" Close

I think it is an opportune time to look into some other ways of closing for commitment, and one method that is closely related to the spirit of the twenty-second close is one that has come to be known as the "Where did I go wrong?" close.

I must say from the beginning that this ploy has a bit of drama associated with it, and maybe this is one of the reasons I find it so much fun to use.

There are two versions available to the "WDIGW" close: (1) the mild version; (2) the strong version. In the mild version, you show a lot of deference to the functionary with whom you are speaking.

"Hello, Mr. Jones? This is Gary Goodman with Goodman Widgets here in Glendale; the reason I'm calling is to understand how you folks normally go about the process of purchasing widgets, because I wouldn't want to misuse your time there, as I know you're busy."

This is a rather "nice and humble" approach, isn't it? It's really an "I-don't-want-to-go-wrong" type of method that compels the listener to shepherd the sale through the gates at the client firm.

This gambit is related to the "Help me out" close, which has the salesperson actually use these words to engineer commitment. Corny as it may sound, when you ask for a person's help, if your plight seems at all reasonable you'll often receive a tremendous degree of assistance simply because you have fashioned your request in this direct way.

The second "Where did I go wrong?" close is pretty dramatic. Imagine you have been trying to sell someone and you just don't seem to be getting anywhere. You can elicit a lot of cooperation by calling the person and saying:

> "Hello, Mr. Smith? This is Gary Goodman with Goodman Insurance; I recognize that we're not doing business as I had once hoped, but I feel that I'll be a much better businessperson if you can help me out by telling me where I went wrong."

Isn't this a nice approach? I'll tell you what I find particularly powerful about it. It disarms the listener by conceding that the battle for his or her business is over. This tells the listener that it's safe to discuss the unsuccessful sales process because it has seen its day and won't be revived.

This approach is also valuable because it creates a sense of commitment on a very human level by implying that the prospect owes it to the salesperson to play the role of coach and offer some valid tips so the seller can shore up his or her powers before meeting the next adversary.

What you find when you use this close is a rather sympathetic reaction on the part of the buyer; so much so that in some cases the buyer will talk him- or herself into giving some sort of order to the salesperson after all, so he or she won't go away empty-handed.

No matter what happens, this kind of post-battle effort *is* a learning experience, and you can sharpen your methods by using a style that seems to be very different from that with which we may be most familiar.

Read This Section Now, or Miss a Golden Opportunity!

Urgency plays a vital role in the closing process. To put it very simply, if people don't think they have to act right away, they won't.

Most of us procrastinate, and nowhere is this habit more prevalent then when a seller is trying to encourage someone to become a buyer. "I'll think it over" is one of the most depressing responses you can hear as a salesperson, unless you have developed a method for taking the sting out of it.

For instance, let's imagine that a buyer tells you that he or she will think it over. You have several responses you can make. One, which isn't productive, is to agree, hang up, and hope that the next person you find won't be as difficult to persuade.

A better response is to say something like this: "And you should think it over, Ms. Jones; however, there simply isn't the kind of time to do that, so we'll take care of this for you, and I know you'll be pleased, okay?"

That's right, *there isn't time*. To create urgency, you need to restrict the amount of time available for deliberation and action. I am aware of telephone rooms that have been using urgency pitches for years, to dramatic effect. Some of their salespeople use what is called a "mis-shipment pitch," which operates very boldly on the basis of urgency. Their presentation sounds something like this:

> "Mr. Jones, this is Bill Smith with XRG Office Supply in Hollywood, and we're on the phone with you because we have a little problem and we know you can help us out.
>
> "By the way, you're still using electrical tape there, aren't you? Well, great. You see, I just sent out three boxes of the half-inch tape to one of my clients there in Hammond, and after I put them on the truck I heard that they had filed for bankruptcy.
>
> "Now, the shipment's already on its way, but I may be able to reroute it to you, and if I can I'll give the tape to you for only $2 a

roll, which is half price, and there are only three gross to a box, all right?"

I'm not very fond of this ploy, and I'm convinced that you can be completely forthright and honest and do a great job in selling, which will make mis-shipment pitches unnecessary. Nonetheless, this ploy works, and it does so because listeners find appeals to urgency nearly irresistible.

If you haven't built a certain amount of urgency into your presentations, you are doing yourself a great disservice while encouraging prospects to stall in their deliberations.

The Inoculation Close

When you come to think about it, most people who buy from you are pretty savvy. They realize that many of us have competitors, and in trying to be prudent buyers they'll most likely try to get in touch with them to perform price/performance comparisons.

All of this is reasonable, and if you are a smart seller you'll anticipate this behavior and build it into your sales talks. For instance, if you know that a prospect is going to hang-up with you and immediately call one of your competitors, you should "inoculate" that prospect with a little bit of the "disease" that he or she will be exposed to upon calling them to make him or her "immune" to their efforts at persuasion.

Here's how it works:

"You'll probably want to check around to see that you're getting the best possible deal from us, right? Well, fine. Who are you going to call next? Oh, I see. Well, you'll probably come across Smith Construction sooner or later, and they're a fine firm, but I've been told that they tend to be on the high side, and when you speak to Hastings Construction, make sure to tell them that the job has to be done on time or you'll assess them a 5-percent penalty for each day over target they get, okay?"

This gives you a feeling for inoculation selling in action. What you're doing is not making any unseemly slams at the competition, but rather pointing out negative features that the customer will want to evaluate as he or she converses with them.

Typically, the average customer will contact one or two competitors at most, verify the concerns you have mentioned, and come running back to you to close the deal. As long as you handle the delicate process of inoculation with a degree of care, you'll find that this tool serves you very well, while positioning you as the customer's friend and consultant.

The fifth 10 seconds in review:

1. Closing is a winning habit, and you should be closing at various points throughout the call to condition the prospect to responding affirmatively when you close during the fifth ten seconds.
2. An excellent closing question to use when a prospect is wavering is: "What's the alternative?"
3. Three closes that work beautifully over the phone are:
   - The assumptive close.
   - The checkback close.
   - The choice close.
4. With some "driving" types of prospects, you'll want to use *unobtrusive closing* techniques.
5. Avoid creating too much *disinformation* during your subtle closes because this can result in the prospect's becoming confused.
6. Create client involvement with your presentation by utilizing the *twenty-second talk* I have developed.
7. Use the "where have I gone wrong?" close to revive lost sales.
8. Build *urgency* into your closes to avoid excuses and stalls, and to pique the interest of the prospect.
9. In competitive situations, use the *inoculation close* to prepare your prospect for encountering your adversaries.

7

The Final 10 Seconds
Sealing the Deal

To the inexperienced seller, the word "okay" signifies that the sales process has come to a successful conclusion when it passes from the lips of an agreeable prospect. This isn't necessarily true, as painful experience has pointed out.

Just because a prospect says "okay" to you doesn't mean that the deal is sealed. On the contrary, this can be anything from an easy way to get you off the phone to someone's attempt to put you on. In other words, creating commitment through the closing process, which we discussed in the last chapter, is just one of two parts to the ultimate decision-making process. Once you have achieved commitment, you need to move swiftly to secure the understanding at which you have arrived.

It is during these final ten seconds of the telemarketing procedure that you need to sound extremely smooth and confident to overcome any reluctance on the part of the listener to go along with the deal.

Fighting Post-Decisional Dissonance

A very natural reaction on the part of a buyer who has just given us her consent is to question the desirability of his or her decision.

This is known as post-decisional dissonance, which means simply that after any decision of consequence most of us become concerned about the attractiveness of the unchosen alternatives in the situation.

Imagine that you're about to have some dessert in a cafeteria. As you pass the "goodies" case, you spy some delicious chocolate cake, and tell yourself, "That looks good!" Next, you spot some Jello and say, "Now, I really *should* have that, instead." After deliberating on the tradeoffs involved in calories and taste, you decide upon the Jello, take it to your seat, begin to eat it, and then decide, "I think I should have had the cake after all."

What's the moral to this story? You can't have your cake and Jello, too. Just kidding ... this illustration points out that we're never completely satisfied with buying decisions we make, and what we need to do is obtain reassurance from salespeople that we have made a proper decision in buying something in the first place.

Help the Customer to Rationalize His or Her Decision

A very important role that a salesperson plays for the buyer is that of a friend who will help the buyer to justify his of her decision in the eyes and minds of third parties. I see this need emerge among corporate buyers all the time.

Corporate buyers may feel very positive about going ahead with a particular project, but they won't make any headway in our direction until you can show them how to make their behavior seem totally coherent to both themselves and their superiors.

The time to do this is immediately after the customer has assented to the proposal. When you hear the magic word "yes," or "okay," you should seek to confirm the understanding right away, and to do so you should follow at least six steps:

1. You should reward the person for her decision.
2. You should confirm delivery details.
3. You should confirm financial details.
4. You should provide for unanswered questions.
5. You should sense any discomfort with the decision.

6. You should leave the buyer feeling good about you.

Let's examine these six steps in the confirmation process in detail to better understand how each one contributes to the stability of the sale.

Rewarding the Buyer

When a person gives us the go-ahead on a deal, he or she tends to feel somewhat out in the cold, all alone, and very vulnerable, unless you come to the rescue and tell the customer that he or she made a good and wise decision after all.

This can be done with very few words. The timing of this message is crucial, though. Just after someone has agreed to a proposal you need to secure the commitment by saying something like, "great," "fine," or "very good." You are free to choose your own favored words of support and encouragement here, but no matter which ones you elect, you'll always want to offer something to bolster the person's decision.

Needless to say, you can go overboard here and actually jeopardize the deal by seeming too eager. For instance, you shouldn't launch into a "You won't regret this" sort of speech, as this can make the person wonder if he or she really shouldn't be regretting the arrangement at this point.

Your tone should be mildly enthusiastic, yet it should reassure the listener by suggesting, "You've made a sound decision here, and you can feel secure that countless others have made the same decision as well."

Confirming Delivery Details

Often, your sale will require you send the product or written contract to the customer, which means that it is only natural to check the delivery details with the person to assure accuracy.

By checking delivery details, you also serve another, more subtle, purpose. This function is really mundane, and it is the sort of informational exchange that isn't subject to being contested by the purchaser. In fact, it is really unlikely that your buyer will interrupt you when you are reciting something as basic as his or her address, and this is a good thing, because you want the person to be cementing the order at this point in the call.

My language in the confirmation will go as follows, as I am going over delivery details:

> "Fine, Ms. Smith, just so I'm clear, I'll be getting those widgets out to you in a week or so, and I show you folks at 229 Jericho Turnpike, Mineola, New York, 22173, is that right? Well, fine."

The assumption we are operating on at this point in the call is that customers *will* interrupt us if they aren't happy with the sale, and if they actually help us to send the widgets to them by confirming basic delivery details, they are giving additional assent to the sale.

Confirming Financial Details

While some sellers disagree with me on this point, I believe it is crucial to the strength of your order to confirm the financial details of your agreement. Too often, buyers don't pay attention to the dollar value of the agreement, only to be shocked later on when they are invoiced for what seems to be an outrageous amount.

You can prevent this "sticker shock" by walking the person through the financial details once again as you confirm the entire deal. Remember this: If they can't reaffirm the money involved with their eyes open to all the facts, then you don't really have a deal in the first place.

This is the time when you need to express just the right attitude with your voice. You need to be really calm and in control as you say:

> "And we're looking at three gross of the electric blue widgets at $99 apiece, for a total of forty-two thousand, seven hundred sixty, plus the standard shipping and handling fees, which run about three hundred."

I know figures such as these can sound awfully stark, but there really isn't any other satisfactory method for going over the money value of the deal without biting the bullet in this manner.

I will say this: When the buyer casually grunts his or her

assent and makes it sound as if the dollars aren't really that much after all, it is a very good feeling to know that he or she is walking into the agreement with both eyes open.

What happens if you don't "go for the wallet" in this manner? It becomes really easy for the buyer to plead insanity or ignorance or to make the excuse of being unaware that he or she had agreed to a deal in the first place. As you can imagine, this can get very costly when you have already gone to the expense of shipping a lot of gizmos all the way across the continent or the world based upon a weak "okay."

It's much better to quash a deal before it gets out the door than to try to remedy things after it is too late. Remember, if you are doing the kind of professional job that telemarketing requires, you aren't ever afraid to get down to basics and create clarity when it comes to money matters.

Provide for
Unanswered Questions

Most new salespeople are treated to various war stories and fables about the selling game. One of the most widespread cautions that a new person will hear has to do with "overtalking," or the habit of talking oneself right out of a deal.

In fact, I recall hearing dozens of experienced salespeople rail against talking after one has attempted a close. These pros have argued that "silence" is the great salesman when the chips are down and you are looking into the poker face that is represented by the prospect sitting in front of you.

There may be something to be said for this concept when you are in the presence of a contract-signing buyer, but when you are on the phone, silence can create uncertainty and cause confusion in both parties to the call.

Instead of avoiding customer questions, I train people to solicit them. What this does is assure the buyer that you are secure and open in your approach, which enhances the buyer's confidence in you. Furthermore, by asking if there are any questions, you have a very important chance to straighten out misunderstandings before they become costly snafus.

After restating the financial details, I simply ask:

"Do you have any questions I can help you with?"

The phrasing of this question is important because you want to express that you are open to feedback at this point. If you used a more harsh approach and asked, "Are there any questions," you might give the impression that you really don't want to hear any, although you have to pay lip service to the issue.

You should be totally prepared to handle 95 percent of the questions that prospects may throw at you. Make sure to have the questions and answers expertly scripted so that there will be little hesitation between the inquiry and the response. Again, this will make you appear self-confident and professional.

In those cases where the question leads you to discuss negative points, or concepts that seem at all on the sour side, remember to answer the question as positively as you can, and then try to take the sting out of the matter by inserting a positive statement directly following your answer.

For instance, if the customer asks:

"Weren't you folks having quality-control problems with the electric blue widgets some time ago?"

Your response might be:

"While it's true that we did have some quality-control challenges a while back, this has been rectified to the point where our defects level is one of the lowest in the industry, and we're really proud of our record of customer satisfaction. Are there any other questions I can help you with?"

Note how I got back on track by asking if there were any *other* questions I could handle for the customer. What this does is tell the person that I think the first question has been handled satisfactorily, and we're ready at this point to push on to other business. This ploy helps you to control the conversation and keep things moving along at a healthy pace.

Sense any Discomfort with the Deal

You're never going to make everyone completely happy with your goods and services, even if you bend over backwards to do so. You could be selling the best chocolate chip cookies in the universe, and someone will knock your product because he or she doesn't like your success, or because he or she claims that your recipe is "too rich" or too chocolatey.

Even if you can't produce total commercial bliss in everyone with whom you speak, you should still try to arrest any obvious dissatisfaction that someone may have with the deal that he or she has made with you. The best time to do this, of course, is before the call has terminated.

Some buyers are so timid that they won't volunteer their dissatisfaction but will instead try to communicate it to you through a negative tone of voice. This requires you to be particularly sensitive to vocal nuances that might indicate that you have an unhappy customer on your hands.

Surprisingly, *some customers can sound too easy* as you are moving through the last ten seconds of the call. They may be "stringing us along" with pleasant affirmative grunts such as "uh huh," and "okay," and the like, when in fact, they have no intention of making a contract at all.

You don't have to worry about hearing negativity from these people, because this isn't their style. On the contrary, they'll lead you on with a hollow sort of pleasantry which lulls you into feeling you have something solid with them when you don't.

Treat them in the same fashion as you would someone who communicates that he or she has a little heartburn with the arrangement you have laid out before him or her. If someone seems unduly "light and airy" or cynical, stop and ask the person:

"Are you *sure* you don't have any questions I can help you with?"

This added probe usually shakes the person up a bit and brings forth any hidden negativity. Sometimes I go a few steps further, actually jeopardizing what might seem to be a solid order by asking:

"Well, Mr. Jones, when you receive the widgets, there won't be anything standing in the way of your remitting a check to us right away, is that right?"

If the person ratifies the deal by indicating that he or she knows his or her assent is creating a financial obligation, I go ahead and process the order. If he balks after hearing this qualifying question, I try to overcome the issues in question and seal the deal.

Try to Distinguish
Questions from Objections

When someone asks a question during the last ten seconds, it can seem like an objection, and sometimes it is. For the most part, though, when a prospect throws a question your way, he or she is really saying, "Please clear up this one area for me, and I'll give you my approval."

If you are handling a question, the procedure is to: (1) Answer the question; (2) Make a positive statement if the answer leaves the issue on a sour note; (3) Ask if there are any other questions you can answer for the prospect.

When you are responding to an objection that comes during the last ten seconds, you should: (1) Answer the objection; (2) Make a positive statement; (3) Close the deal again.

You'll notice that you have to close another time if the customer's objection strikes at the very heart of the deal, which it may do if the person says that he or she thinks the entire proposal is "too expensive." If you fail to properly address the issue and close again for commitment, you'll be sure to lose the deal.

However, beware of the "boomerang effect;" don't fall into the trap of closing a person again if he or she is only asking you a "friendly" question. This will make you seem unduly jittery and insecure, and it could cost you the deal.

Leave the Buyer
Feeling Good About You

A telephone sale is very much like a circle: you start the call with a certain amount of friendliness and good will, and if you do your job well you'll end it on the same note of good cheer and optimism.

This requires that you consciously attempt to elevate the buyer's mood at the end of the call by making some kind of *personal contact* with the person that seems to transcend your interest in making an agreement.

I like to say something like this:

> "Well, I want to thank you for your time *and* your patience, and I'll look forward to speaking with you again soon. 'Bye."

This short thank-you can take the chill off a transaction and make the person feel that I have genuine gratitude for his or her business. This type of sentence usually enables me to hear the person's voice again, as many people chime in at this point with a little laughter or with some feedback such as, "Nice talking with you, too," or something of this sort.

Programming Future Orders

The last ten seconds represents a good time to "program" your customers to give you repeat business. What you can do is alert people to the fact that you will be getting back to them on a regular basis to handle their orders for them, and this can lead to their giving you more of their business in the future.

The last 10 seconds in review:
1. When you have closed an order you shouldn't rush off the phone. Instead, you should set forth to solidify the agreement you have made.
2. You need to fight buyer's remorse, or post-decisional dissonance, which is the customer's tendency to become concerned about the merit of a buying decision he or she has just made.
3. A part of the role of the seller is to help the buyer to rationalize or justify his or her buying decision. This is accomplished through a six-part process:
   * You reward the buyer for his or her decision.
   * You confirm delivery details.
   * You confirm financial details.
   * You provide for unanswered questions.
   * You sense any discomfort with the buying decision.
   * You leave the buyer feeling good about you.

4. It is important to distinguish questions from objections. They must be treated differently.
5. During the last ten seconds you can program future orders by alerting the customer to the fact that you'll be calling at regular intervals for his or her business

Afterword

Thank you for reading *Gary Goodman's 60-Second Salesperson*.

This is the fifth volume in my Telephone Effectiveness Library™, and I certainly enjoyed the challenge of writing this new book.

Some of my other titles you have seen in these pages are *Winning by Telephone; Reach Out & Sell Someone; Selling Skills for the Nonsalesperson;* and *You Can Sell Anything by Telephone!*

I am committed to bringing you the most useful information to be found anywhere in the field of telemarketing and management. By the time you have read this book, my sixth volume will be in press. It is *Breakthroughs in Telemarketing & Management.*

Please let me know of your successes and challenges as you meet the task of selling and training others to sell. I find that I learn a great deal through reader feedback and through the seminars that I offer from time to time across the country.

If you are interested in learning more about these training sessions, or if you wish to explore the prospect of having my firm develop a telemarketing program for your organization, please contact me at the address below, and we'll follow up with you.

If you are interested in receiving a sample issue of the

monthly "Telephone Effectiveness Newsletter," along with information regarding our complete line of audio-cassette training libraries and books, please send $5 to cover costs to our address, and ask for the "Infopak."

I wish you the very best, and I look forward to hearing from you.

Gary S. Goodman, Ph.D.
President
Goodman Communications Corporation
P.O. Box 9733
Glendale, California 91206
(818) 243-7338

Index